5 Secrets of Health and Happiness

5 Secrets of Health and Happiness

Chinese Wisdom to Nourish Your Life

Angela Hicks

Thorsons

Thorsons
An Imprint of HarperCollins*Publishers*
77–85 Fulham Palace Road,
Hammersmith, London W6 8JB

The Thorsons website address is: www.thorsons.com

Originally published by Thorsons in 1998 as
The 5 Laws of Healthy Living
This edition published by Thorsons 2001

1 3 5 7 9 10 8 6 4 2

A catalogue record for this book
is available from the British Library

ISBN 0 00 711069 3

Printed and bound in Great Britain by
Martins the Printers Limited, Berwick upon Tweed

Contents

Author's Note

I have capitalized all Chinese medical terminology in this book in order to differentiate it from standard English terms.

My thanks to all of the people who have helped me to write this book.

I'd firstly like to thank the practitioners and patients who have been so willing to talk to me and/or fill in questionnaires. They are: Sue Bishop, Simon Blyth, Stevie Charlton, Lydia Coles, Deb Cosbey, Jennifer Dale, Flora Dowling, Helen Fielding, Lucy Fox, Julia Funk, Justin Hextall, Sue Horne, Wayne Howe, Bill Jaeger, Stella King, Magda Koc, Gio Maschio, Frances Mason, David Mayor, Carey Morgan, Gail Newton, Philippa Nice, Sue Pready, Colin Reader, Amanda Rolt, Jackie Shaw, Joanne Sherwin, Beth Soderstrom, Deborah Thomson, Alison West, Diane Wheatley and Geraldine Worthington.

All patients' names have been changed for confidentiality.

Secondly, I'd also like to thank the people who have read through this book and commented on it. Especially Judith Clark for correcting each new chapter and giving me many good ideas. Peter Mole for his advice as well as help with the overview. Also Gaby Hock and Jane Grossfeld for reading the book and making extremely helpful suggestions and to Val Kennedy for reading the rewritten book.

I'd also like to thank Wanda Whiteley from Thorsons – her expert guidance has enabled me to shape the book into its final form.

Finally, I'd also like to thank my husband John whose love and encouragement has supported me throughout the time I've written this book.

Introduction

I can still remember when I first studied Chinese medicine. As I learned parts of the theory such as Yin and Yang, Qi energy and the Five Elements, my perspective on life was totally transformed.

I found one particular part of the theory especially fascinating and empowering. It was the knowledge of what causes disease and how we can remain healthy. Here was a viewpoint about the prevention of disease which was sensible and totally new to me. Here also were principles which I could immediately apply in my life.

Before studying Chinese medicine I had never really thought about why we become ill. Like many other people I had assumed that some people were merely 'unlucky' and became unhealthy, whilst others were more fortunate and managed to stay well. Health seemed to be a game of chance.

Times are changing. Thankfully, many people now understand that there are always underlying causes to their illnesses and that they can participate in their own well-being. The Chinese, however, are one of the few cultures who have preserved accurate knowledge about how to stay healthy. They have documented advice in such a way that it is easy to follow. By following it, we have a better chance of remaining well throughout our lives.

It is interesting to note that Chinese people tend to place a higher priority on maintaining their health than do Western people. A survey carried out by the office of Population Censuses and Surveys in England in 1993 illustrates the benefits they gain from their attitude[1]. This research found that only 29%

of Chinese pensioners have serious and long-lasting illnesses, compared to 36% of white people and 43% of people of Indian or Pakistani origin. These statistics are truly stunning – especially bearing in mind that most of the people included in this census were living in an unfamiliar culture. In China itself, we might expect the results to have been even more spectacular.

My fascination with Chinese medicine has never left me and I am equally driven by the desire to let others know about this important practice. This book describes many useful ways in which Chinese people keep themselves well. It is written in the form of five 'secrets' for health and happiness. Understanding these secrets will enable us to improve and maintain our health and prevent many illnesses in the future.

As a teacher and practitioner of Chinese medicine, I often hear stories of patients who have improved their health enormously or who are now maintaining good health having changed some aspects of their lifestyle. In this book I have drawn many examples from these people. I have either talked to them personally or asked them to fill in a questionnaire. Some people have gained this lifestyle advice from an acupuncturist, herbalist or other Chinese medicine practitioner. They realize that going to a practitioner for treatment can be an important step when we are ill. If, however, we only have treatment 'done to us' and go back to the lifestyle that has made us sick, we may not stay well.

This book is for all of us who want to sustain our health. It will provide guidelines to enable us to do so.

Why a Healthy Lifestyle?

What is the meaning of 'good health'? Some people think they are healthy if they have no illnesses. Someone told me the other day, 'I don't get colds and infections and I have no physical symptoms. The doctor says that I'm healthy, so I must be.'

But does this person *feel* well? To decide, a practitioner of Chinese medicine would also want to ask some other questions, such as:

- Do you usually feel vital and energetic?
- Can you sustain your energy for most of the day?
- Are you mentally and emotionally positive and happy to be alive?

If the answer to these questions is generally 'Yes', then a person is well on the way to being healthy on all levels – not just physically, but mentally and spiritually.

If the answer to any of these three questions is 'No', then there is much that can be done. We can read this book and discover the secrets written within it. These secrets have been known in the East for thousands of years.

We can also use the questionnaire at the end of the book (*see page 212*) to re-evaluate our lifestyles, then follow the Seven Step Plan for Healthy Living on page 206. This will direct us towards becoming healthier, having a better quality of life *and* maintaining it.

Even if some of us answered 'Yes' to these questions, we can still ask ourselves, 'Am I leading a lifestyle that will *sustain* my health in the future or have I just been lucky so far?'

A patient who now has diabetes, once said to me:

> I used to think I was healthy. I drank too much, ate badly, stayed up too late and overworked – I didn't think it mattered. If I'd known when I was 25 what I now know about lifestyle, I'd have lived completely differently. My lifestyle was atrocious and I've often wondered if I could have prevented getting diabetes later in life.

This patient is now in her 50s and she will never know if her diabetes could have been avoided. At 25, however, if she'd re-evaluated all aspects of her lifestyle, it would have helped her to take stock of her life. She could then have worked towards restoring herself to a healthier equilibrium – this would certainly have reduced her chances of subsequently becoming diabetic.

You too might consider whether you are living a lifestyle that will sustain your health and happiness in the future.

A healthy lifestyle will help us to:

1   get better when we are ill
2   prevent illnesses before they happen
3   feel in peak condition both mentally and physically.

Some people think it will be difficult to alter their lifestyles or don't know where to start. This book will provide you with the knowledge to help you make the adjustments best suited to your needs. In the rest of this chapter we'll consider many of the most common issues which concern people who are considering adjusting their lifestyles. These include:

1   why a healthy lifestyle is important
2   what the benefits are
3   how we can achieve a healthy lifestyle.

Firstly, how does ill-health originate?

Why we become ill

Although we can't avoid all diseases, we do know that every illness has a cause. The Chinese describe these causes as:

1   dietary causes
2   emotional causes
3   imbalances of work, rest and exercise
4   climatic causes
5   constitutional causes.

Each of these areas is covered by one of the Five Secrets in this book.

The consequences of an unhealthy lifestyle often take time to emerge – we can be damaging our health without knowing it. A bad diet, for example, may take years before producing a symptom. The practice of a healthy lifestyle is important. Prevention means acting *before* the problems manifest.

Can I Avoid Getting Ill if I Live Healthily?

Some illnesses can easily be avoided while others are more difficult to prevent.

Illnesses which are easily prevented

Most people in the West don't realize how devastating the weather can be to our health. The Chinese understand simple ways of preventing these bad effects. For example, if we remain in wet clothes after we're caught in the rain, then the Damp can penetrate. This can lead to a bad cold. It can also penetrate deeper and cause other problems such as joint conditions, a muzzy headache, poor concentration or feeling depressed. Once we understand that it is important to change out of wet clothes we can escape these harmful repercussions. In Chapter 5 we will discuss other simple ways of avoiding the effects of the weather.

Most of us also make choices with regard to the balance of our work, rest and exercise. If, for example, we work without rest for long periods then we can get worn out and may succumb to illnesses more easily. If we then don't convalesce, the consequences may be even more severe. Illness such as post-viral syndrome, constant colds and flu, anxiety, tiredness, depression and many other conditions, may be due to overworking when we should be resting. By changing lifestyle habits these illnesses are preventable.

Events we can't predict

Life will never be totally predictable, however, and other causes are less easy to avoid. Stresses like deaths, accidents and other emotional traumas can't be avoided and can certainly take their toll on our health. We can compare a healthy lifestyle to taking out an insurance policy. Good lifestyle habits will enable us to cope better through an unexpected crisis and will take us a long way towards preventing illness in the future.

We've taken a glimpse at Chinese medicine in relation to illness. Now let's look at it in relation to health. To understand the Chinese view of health, we need to find out more about Qi energy.

Chinese Medicine and our Energy

Chinese medicine teaches us that our health is dependent on the balance of the Qi energy in our bodies. Qi is our life force. When we have abundant Qi which is flowing smoothly around our system then we are healthy physically, mentally and spiritually. When our energy is deficient or blocked, we become unhealthy.

Although Qi cannot be seen, it nevertheless penetrates every cell of our body allowing us to feel, think, move and have vitality. When we die the Qi has left our body and the life force has gone. A lifestyle which enhances our Qi will sustain our health. If we live a lifestyle that weakens or blocks our Qi then we lose our health.

Chinese Medicine and Health

Practitioners of Chinese medicine look at the balance of each person's Qi and view each individual as a whole – this includes their environment and lifestyle.

Most of us now know that lifestyle affects our health but we are still orientated towards a Western viewpoint of disease. If we have something 'wrong' with us, we expect a pill to take it away. When we go to a doctor they often feel obliged to hand us a prescription. If this doesn't work, then we haven't had the right thing 'done' to us.

In comparison, practitioners of Chinese medicine assess each individual as a whole and look for the cause of a person's problem. They understand that a Western drug will only take away a symptom. This will bring temporary improvement but won't deal with the underlying cause, so we can expect the symptom to return or a new symptom to appear later. Chinese medicine understands the true 'pill' – we need to adapt our lifestyle to support our health and happiness.

Is this Just Another Fad?

Many people get confused because they hear so many conflicting guidelines about health. I met someone who once worked for a well-known health magazine. He told me:

> What we think is healthy goes in and out of fashion and we never get it
> completely right. There's always something new that comes along and we
> end up not knowing which advice to trust.

It's no wonder that these lifestyle secrets might mistakenly be called another fad. What makes them different is that they are workable rules that are still used throughout Chinese society today. They have stood the test of time and have been handed down through Chinese families for thousands of years. They are backed up by many historical texts which go back over 2,000 years.

Lifestyle in Chinese history

The most famous Chinese medical textbook of all is called *The Yellow Emperor's Classic of Internal Medicine* and it was written in 200 BC. This book lays down the foundation of all Chinese medicine used today. It also gives much dietary advice and says that proper food and drink should form the basis for the treatment of all disease and illness.

Huang Fu Mi

Another notable text is *The Compendium of Acupuncture and Moxibustion*. This was written by a doctor called Huang Fu Mi (pronounced Hwang Foo Mee) who was born in AD 215. As well as having much to say about acupuncture treatment in his book, he also presents a teaching with which many of us will agree. He says that preventative treatment is the highest form of medicine and that the best treatment is performed before a disease has manifested.

Sun Si Miao

A doctor called Sun Si Miao (pronounced Sun See Me-ow) also commented on the benefits of living a healthy lifestyle. He lived during the Tang dynasty which was between AD 582 and 682. This great Chinese doctor, who is sometimes known as 'the father of Chinese medicine', described many important rules of hygiene which were based on breathing and diet. He distinguished himself in diseases caused by malnutrition and he used diet as a medical therapy. Sun Si Miao said that first we should change our lifestyle to become healthy. If these lifestyle changes didn't work then we should use acupuncture or other forms of Chinese medicine.

Health fads

Health fads often look at health from a short-term view. In contrast, these Chinese traditions provide a long-term perspective on our health and are as relevant today as they were 2,000 years ago.

So why did the Chinese preserve this rich understanding of health while we in the West have lost much of this knowledge? The answer lies in motivation.

The Chinese and Longevity

Chinese society has traditionally placed a high value on longevity. People have looked forward to their old age and have therefore been strongly motivated towards cultivating good health.

Respect for the old

The best way to send our good wishes to a Chinese person is to wish them 'a long and healthy life'. It is understood that with age comes wisdom. In Chinese families the oldest member is traditionally shown great respect and their opinions are highly valued.

At one time we too respected our old people. Times have changed. Now many old people feel discarded and dismissed in their later years and the wisdom they have accumulated is ignored. Keeping well by living a healthy lifestyle is now perhaps all the more essential. A healthy lifestyle may enable us to cope with whatever life presents us – including our old age.

Our motivation for staying healthy

The motivation to maintain health and longevity has been ingrained in Chinese culture for thousands of years. From generation to generation people studied how they were affected by their lifestyle. The results were then passed on through further generations, who continued the study. We saw in the Introduction that Chinese pensioners in the West are significantly healthier than their Western counterparts – this is hardly surprising when we realize how motivated they are to maintain their health.

Lifestyle in 'Modern' Times

Changes over the last 50 years have had an effect on our health. Let's look at some of these.

1 Our society, which was previously a farming society, has become increasingly industrialized and the nature of work has changed. Many people are now working in factories doing repetitive work or are working in offices where they are doing mental work with very little physical activity.
2 Information technology has revolutionized communication so that we can see the latest film in our living room, send e-mails across the globe, shop on-line, find information on the Internet or chat to friends on our mobile phones.

3 Electric lighting means we can now work or shop 24 hours a day.

4 Improved transport means we can fly to another continent for a holiday or drive to work.

5 Science has transformed food processing using preservatives and colorings to make food longer lasting, attractive looking and easier to prepare.

Lifestyle in the West before Industrialization

Before the industrial revolution of the early 19th century, most people's lifestyles were very different. They lived in harmony with the cycles of nature as had their ancestors for generations before them. People rose when it became light and worked until darkness fell. In the winter they spent more time sleeping because it was darker for longer and in the summer they were awake until later and rose earlier. There was no electricity to keep people alert after darkness fell, no television or films to keep them stimulated and no telephones to chat with friends.

Our natural rhythms

We can now have light for 24 hours a day, changing our natural rhythms and subsequently our health. Although we don't wish to go back to times before electricity, we should be aware of our natural waking and sleeping times during the seasons and harmonize with them.

Once people worked in the fields and looked after their animals and crops. The crops would feed their families and others close to them and people would naturally eat the food that grew around them in the different seasons. In the autumn, food was stored to last through the long winter months and in the summer, more fresh food could be eaten. Flavoring, colorings and additives did not exist and at that time no one could have imagined that animals would be factory-farmed, acres of crops sprayed with chemicals or food genetically modified.

Exercising and work

Two centuries ago, a majority of the work was physical – this meant that most people exercised as they worked. Looking after crops, storing food, doing various household tasks, pulling carts and riding horses were some of the various activities carried out on a daily basis. Nowadays, farm work is mostly done by machine and many of us sit in an office all day in front of a computer. If we want to exercise we have to make time for it and many of us fail to get any significant physical activity at all.

At one time when people needed to travel they usually walked or rode horses. Even 50 years ago, very few people owned a car and cycling and walking were the main modes of transport. We now take it for granted that we can travel thousands of miles by airplane. What would have previously been a two-day journey on foot now takes an hour in the car.

Adapting to the 21st Century

Most of us would prefer not to go back to the lifestyle of 50 years ago. The changes have brought with them many benefits as well as disadvantages.

One of the benefits is that we live more varied lifestyles. We have a greater choice of food in our diet and have labor-saving devices to do strenuous tasks. This leaves many people with the chance to have much more leisure time – though ironically it is increasingly common for people to overwork. Our world has expanded enormously – we can now watch what is happening all over the world on the television, contact friends in many countries at the touch of a button and regularly travel abroad.

Our attitude to our lifestyle

One of the biggest disadvantages is our attitude to our lifestyle. For example, in the area of work, some people overwork and override their feelings of tiredness. Many get sick, then work through their illnesses instead of resting and convalescing. Others are juggling more than one job and women (and now more frequently men too) are often torn between the needs of family and work. The more we overwork, the more difficult we may find it to stop. Financial demands, pressures from the work-team and desire for promotion can all add to the stress. The occurrence of illness continues to rise.

Diet

Our diets have also changed – many people now eat diets which do not nourish them, skip meals frequently or eat irregularly. Others get very little exercise. They may be employed in static jobs having driven to work rather than walked or cycled.

Stress

What is the result of this lack of care for our lifestyles? The result is falling levels of health and well-being. An increasing number of people now view feeling dissatisfied, tired and slightly depressed as a normal way of life. Along with this, the level of illness continues to rise.

Brian Inglis tells us in his book *The Diseases of Civilisation* that compared to the earlier part of this century, there are now an increasing number of days lost from work due to ill-health, more medical drug prescriptions are issued and more people are admitted to hospital. Over half of the men and two thirds of the women interviewed in a survey considered that they had chronic or recurrent health problems.

Illnesses and life expectancy

Even the well-publicized fact that we now have a longer life-expectancy is misleading. This increase is mostly due to people surviving childbirth and infancy because of improved living standards rather than improved general health. There is now an increase in the incidence of many illnesses resulting from modern civilization. These include an increase in heart attacks, cancer, allergies, mental illness and degenerative diseases such as multiple sclerosis.[1] The common situation of TATT (Tired All The Time) and the post-viral syndrome ME (myalic encehalomyelitis) can be added to this list.

One answer to this situation is that we can individually take greater responsibility for our own health and well-being by caring for ourselves.

Being Aware of the Need for a Healthy Lifestyle

When we are ill we need to pay more attention to our health. In reality this is often when we feel least able to cope. We may take as many short cuts as possible. For example, eating 'fast' food makes our lives easier and when our Qi is weak, many people eat poor quality foods. A friend recently commented:

> One thing I've noticed about my eating habits is that if I'm tense and stressed then I tend to eat fatty and sweet food like chocolate bars.

The quality of these foods will further weaken our Qi over a period of time. My friend then went on to say:

> If I give myself the opportunity to do Yoga or Qigong exercises and relax, then the desire to eat these foods goes away. I then end up looking forward to eating a wholesome meal.

Awareness of the consequences of ignoring our body's messages may lead us to make healthy adjustments to our lifestyle. By doing this we can avoid further ill-health and enjoy the benefits of good health and happiness.

The Results of Lifestyle Changes

All of us can benefit from some simple adjustments to our lifestyle. For many, this can mean increased vitality, greater well-being and feeling more contented with our lives.

For others, the improvements will be to do with current problems. These may include digestive and bowel disorders, headaches, joint problems, mental and emotional complaints, circulatory disorders, gynecological conditions, skin diseases, chest complaints and reproductive disorders, to name but a few. By modifying our lifestyle we can expect to feel healthier physically, mentally and spiritually.

The benefits of adjusting our lifestyles

Throughout this book we will hear from numerous people who tell us about the benefits they gained from changing to a healthier lifestyle. Here William recounts some of the changes he made which have had large repercussions for his health:

I had bad skin on my chest, back and face, felt pretty tired in the afternoons and felt fuzzy in my head. After I'd eaten I felt a tightness around my ankles and feet. I cut out tea and coffee as well as pretty much all dairy products and also wheat and bread – although I still had pasta. I started eating three meals a day with no snacking in between.

The first thing I noticed was that I had a headache and I felt lower back pain around my kidney area and my sweat was very strong for about 3–4 days. Also, the first pee in the morning was quite dark. I lost a lot of weight from my belly and sides very quickly. This was a surprise. I'd always thought I had a bit of a tummy and although I'd eaten less, it had been there most of the time. I realized that I'd really been very bloated.

After about a week I felt really clear in my head and my whole body felt much lighter. The tightness round my joints went. Rather than cutting everything out I had one dessert a week – I had an apple and blackberry pie the other day – and 3–4 pints of Guinness every couple of weeks. The better I felt, the more I enjoyed the diet and I didn't find it boring. Because I felt so much better it was easy to keep to what I was eating. My skin completely cleared up in a couple of weeks and I've had no outbreaks on my face at all. I used to feel that my skin was greasy under the surface – now it feels much dryer. It was very dramatic. Best of all I feel so much better about myself now.

Can a Healthy Lifestyle Always Restore my Health?

If we are really ill it is always best to go to a doctor or a practitioner of Chinese medicine such as an acupuncturist or herbalist. Chinese medicine will increase our Qi and help to restore our health. If we do have treatment from a practitioner of Chinese medicine this can then give us the strength to make necessary changes to our lifestyle. We can always benefit from living healthily and keeping ourselves well will then create longer lasting changes in our health.

The extent to which we can heal our illnesses with lifestyle alone depends on our overall constitution, as well as on the severity of our illness.

Do I have to be Perfect?

Sometimes people avoid looking at their lifestyle because they imagine modifying it will take too much effort. William, who earlier talked about the alterations he'd made, kept small 'treats' for himself when he changed his diet. This, combined with noticing that his symptoms had disappeared, made his adjustments a positive experience. It's best that the process of change is a welcome one and that we each do it in our own unique way. We can then feel proud and satisfied that we are doing the best for ourselves. There is no such thing as a 'right' way of living – just some helpful golden rules which can guide us.

In Chapter 8 we will look at what changes we wish to make and how to make alterations which are right for us. This includes considering how to make changes enjoyable, making adjustments as slowly or as quickly as we wish and finding ways to integrate them into our daily life. Writing down a list of the changes we wish to make and giving ourselves as much time as we need to change will help us to successfully make adjustments (*see page 196 for more on this*).

How Long will it Take to Change my Habits?

The Chinese know an important secret about changing a habit. *Changing a habit takes a month.* Whatever the area of our life – whether it's exercise, diet, dealing with our emotions or protecting ourselves from the climate – it always takes a month. Examples of changes might be:

- reducing 'Phlegm' forming foods in our diet
- regularly exercising in the morning

- becoming more positive
- protecting ourselves from the Cold and Damp.

The adjustment might seem difficult for a while, but give it a month to fully make the change. It will then seem natural and the new habit will be integrated into our daily lives.

Our lifestyle requirements vary according to many situations. These include: the seasons, the climate we live in, our age, our general health and our constitution. We can modify our lifestyle according to each of these and be flexible enough to listen to the messages our body and mind give us.

Pat, who has become much healthier over a number of years, wisely said:

> I find that it's a matter of maintaining a gentle discipline, rather than being
> rigid or adding too many things to do.

The most important result of good health is a feeling of well-being and vitality. One sign of this is an additional spring in the step and a shine in the eye. Putting pressure on ourselves will only cause us to feel guilty every time we 'fail' in what we are trying to do.

How to Read this Book

This book will give us guidelines about all aspects of our lives. Some of us may want to read through the Secrets in the order which they find them. Others may wish to start with the Secret which seems most relevant to them. Whichever way you choose to read this book, I hope you gain much from knowing about the Five Secrets of Health and Happiness.

Summary

1 Health is something we experience not only physically, but mentally and spiritually.
2 Over a period of 2,000 years, Chinese medicine has preserved a rich tradition showing us how to remain healthy – it teaches ways of conserving and balancing our Qi. This is in contrast to 'modern' culture where people often override their health needs.

3 Five important areas which we can modify to stay healthy are:
   - diet
   - emotions
   - work, rest and exercise
   - the climate
   - our constitution.

These are dealt with in the following chapters.

4 A healthy lifestyle will help us to maintain good health. It can restore our health if we are unwell. If it doesn't, we may need to get the help of a practitioner of Chinese medicine. Living healthily will then maintain the benefits gained from treatment.
5 We don't have to be 'perfect' to live healthily.
6 It takes a month to completely alter our bad habits.

The Secret of Healthy Eating

Anna is a 24-year-old residential social worker. She found that a change in her diet had a profound effect on her health.

I'd suffered from irritable bowel syndrome for eight years. Then I went to an acupuncturist. He told me I was eating a diet that was too 'Damp' and that I should come off all foods that aggravated my condition. In my case it was mainly cheese and peanuts. I cut out the peanuts and in the first week I felt much better. I then tackled the cheese – I had adored it and cut it down to 1–2 times a week. I found it made a huge difference.

I've now got rid of the irritable bowel syndrome after eight years. I'd had it constantly and repeatedly – I assumed I'd have it for life and it went more or less immediately. Irritable bowel syndrome makes you feel terrible – after two weeks I no longer felt bloated and my bowels were much better. Suddenly I started looking in the mirror and I'd say to myself, 'You're not so bad after all chuck.'

So what secrets have Chinese medicine practitioners known about diet that Anna and many people in the West didn't understand? Was it merely that she was eating an overly rich diet? Yes, that was certainly part of the problem. Large amounts of dairy produce and other fatty food clog up our system and prevent body fluids from moving easily. The Chinese call this 'Damp' because it has many of the characteristics of dampness in nature.

Damp gives us symptoms such as bloating, a feeling of heaviness, a muzzy head and loose bowels – it's a bit like having water-logged earth inside our bodies.

There was more to it than this, however, as Anna was also eating the wrong proportions in her diet. An incorrect balance of food was having a significant effect on her health. It is a common problem for people. In Part 1 of this chapter we will find out more about the importance of the proportions of food we eat and we will look at the effects of these foods. We'll also consider the issue of vegetarianism versus meat eating and how to loose weight without dieting. Part 2 will cover five other significant areas to do with our diet, including more about the what we eat, how we eat and when we eat.

Part One
Balancing Our Diet

If we changed the quantities of each type of food we eat on a daily basis, it could have a profound effect on our health. It might also prevent some major illnesses commonly found in the West.

Research has found that diseases such as coronary heart disease, many cancers such as stomach, colon and breast cancers, gallstones, high blood pressure, goiter, diabetes, osteoporosis and arthritis are all related to the typical Western diet.[1]

Chinese medicine teaches that poor eating habits will negatively affect our health physically, mentally and spiritually. A good diet, on the other hand, gives us a feeling of well-being and energy.

In the West our present diet has deviated far from that eaten by our ancestors. It is hardly surprising that so many of our current health problems are exacerbated by a poor diet. A research paper written on the health of elderly people states that, 'People are often unaware of how much the national diet has changed during the last decades. We can now afford to eat foods every day that our ancestors only had on festive occasions.'[2]

The Correct Proportions of Foods

So what are the proportions that the Chinese typically eat and that our ancestors ate in the past? Food can be divided into three main groups in these quantities:

1 40–45 per cent of grains and carbohydrates – the Chinese typically eat a large amount of rice.
2 35–40 per cent of vegetables as well as some fruit.
3 10–15 per cent of rich foods such as meat, seafood and eggs, dairy products, fats and oils and sugars.

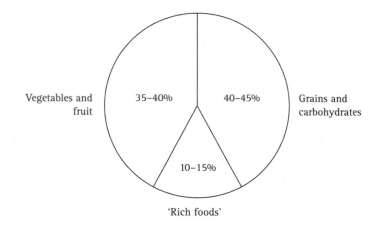

Figure 1: Proportions of food in a well-balanced diet.

As the West has grown more affluent, we have changed the proportions of food we eat until our 'normal' diet has been turned on its head. Westerners eat a diet containing a large amount of rich foods that have strong tastes. We often eat only a small proportion of the grains, beans and vegetables which should be a staple part of our diet.

The Chinese look upon richer foods such as animal products, dairy products and other fats as 'special' and extremely nourishing – but only in small quantities. Excessive amounts of these foods are harder for our system to assimilate. Eaten in greater quantities they will end up upsetting our digestion and the balance of our health. By cutting out cheese and peanuts from her diet Anna not only cut out rich foods, she also changed her whole dietary balance. She describes the actual changes she made on page 28.

Research on the Food Proportions in our Diet

Has there ever been a time when we have eaten more in line with these correct quantities? We can go back to the 1940s when British people were eating a rationed wartime diet. The occurrence of coronary heart disease and many other illnesses were at an all-time low level during this period. Comparing the average British diet in 1948 with more recent years we now eat 50 per cent more meat and twice as much cheese, but less than half as much bread, potatoes and other carbohydrates – an astonishing difference![3] The wartime diet was much closer to the Chinese diet than it is now.

A diet based on grains and vegetables is central to most cultures. Two other well-researched diets are the Japanese diet and the Mediterranean diet.[4,5] These diets were carefully measured during the 1960s and both use similar proportions to the typical Chinese diet. The life expectancy for Greek people who were eating this diet during the 1960s was among the highest in the world.[6] At the same time the rates of many cancers, coronary heart disease and other diet-related chronic illnesses were at their lowest level, despite far more limited medical services than those available today.[7]

The United States Department of Agriculture and the British Health Education Authority (along with the World Health Organization) now recommend a diet using quantities of foods similar to those eaten by the Chinese.[8,9] Let's take a closer look at the proportions of food eaten in a Chinese-style diet.

Grains and beans

Grains and beans need to form about 40–45 per cent of our diet and should be eaten daily. The staple food of Chinese people is of course rice. To achieve variety, rice can be combined with other grains such as wheat in breads and pastas as well as oats, rye, corn and millet. We should, however, be careful about eating too much wheat. Many people in the West overdose on it. As wheat is a very 'Dampening' food (as opposed to rice which clears Dampness from the body), it should be eaten in moderation and not to the exclusion of all other grains (*more about this on page 22*).

Grains can be supplemented by dried beans, such as soya beans and other soya products like tofu. Other beans such as lentils, split peas, adzuki beans, black-eyed beans, chickpeas (garbanzos), mung beans, haricot beans and kidney beans can also be used. All grains and beans should be as un-processed as possible and, like all other foods, organically grown whenever available. For information on how to cook grains and beans see page 220.

Vegetables and fruit

Vegetables, along with some fruits, should provide at least 35–40 per cent of our daily food intake. Vegetables are probably the most neglected part of the Western diet. Some individuals, especially young teenagers, can go for days without eating any plant products at all. This is potentially damaging to their health.

Between 1966 and 1982 a study was carried out in Japan on 270,000 people.[10] The participants in the study ate green or yellow vegetables such as carrots, tomatoes, chicory, spinach, broccoli, leeks, turnip leaves and pumpkins every day. The results of this study found that the risks of cancers, heart disease and many other terminal illnesses were substantially reduced *merely by adding vegetables to the diet*. At the same time this caused aging to slow down by a huge 10–15 years! Fatigue was also considerably lessened as were other stress disorders such as insomnia and irritation.

It is only a small change for us to increase the amount of vegetables on our plates. This study shows that the long-term ramifications should be considerable when we make this simple switch – especially if our vegetables are well prepared.

How Should We Prepare Our Vegetables?

Chinese people are often shocked and mystified when they see people in the West happily eating raw food and vegetables. They would suggest that vegetables should be lightly cooked before eating. There are two main reasons for this.

The first reason is that raw vegetables are harder to digest than cooked ones. Cooking starts to break down the food and aids the Stomach's digestion process. It will also result in more of the food being absorbed. For example, only 50 per cent of a carrot will be absorbed if it is raw compared to 65 per cent of a cooked carrot.[11]

Secondly, and very importantly, practitioners of Chinese medicine understand that the process of digestion requires heat. The Stomach can be compared to a large cooking pot full of soup boiling at 100 degrees centigrade.[12] Putting large amounts of cold food into this soup will cool it down substantially and so require more energy to break it down. Long-term eating of raw vegetables and cold food may make us very lethargic due to the extra energy we need to digest it. Derek, who had bowel problems, changed to eating warmer food:

> My practitioner told me to eat more warm foods. When he said it I realized that I've always preferred warm foods and that when I had salads and other cold foods all day then I didn't feel right and my bowels were worse. He explained that if I had cold food I should have something hot as well to balance it. I felt better for the change and much less tired.

Our ancestors recognized the importance of eating warm food. An old saying that was often quoted said that we should 'eat at least one hot meal a day'. Many of us have now forgotten this sensible piece of advice and eat cold food throughout the day, even in the middle of winter. Adding at least a hot soup to our diet and cooking our vegetables can make a substantial difference.

Meat, fish, poultry, eggs, dairy produce, fats and sugars

These are all classed as 'rich' foods by the Chinese and should be eaten only in small quantities. Good quality animal products, dairy products and oily foods are very nourishing but they only need to form 10–15 per cent of our diet.

We can compare eating large amounts of these rich foods to taking 10 times the prescribed dose of a medicine. We might think that a larger dose will improve our health 10 times as much as a normal dose – of course we will really be taking a dangerous overdose.

Phlegm and Damp-forming Foods

One result of overdosing on rich food is the formation of 'Phlegm' and 'Damp' in our systems. Earlier Anna spoke about symptoms she experienced from eating too much of these foods (*see page 16*). Symptoms can include bloating and bowel disorders such as loose bowels, as well as chronic blocked sinuses, phlegm in the chest, heavy limbs, achy joints and one common problem of our time – obesity. A lack of concentration, tiredness, a muzzy head or even depression can also occur. If you recognize that you have some of these symptoms and suspect you have Phlegm and Damp, below is a list of the foods which may exacerbate your condition.

Which foods cause Phlegm and Damp?

Some of the most common 'Damp' and 'Phlegm' forming foods are:

- dairy produce – milk, butter, cheese, cream etc.
- fatty foods including fatty meat and fried foods
- sugar and sweeteners
- wheat – in excess – including breads and pasta
- concentrated juices such as orange juice, tomato purée
- peanuts, bananas, excessive alcohol.

You might notice that many (but not all) of the foods listed above are 'sticky' in nature. We can start to notice the varying effect different foods have on our systems. For many of us *reducing* rather than completely cutting out these foods will help to clear our systems. For others – particularly if we easily form Phlegm and Damp in our systems – it may be best to completely cut these foods from our diet, at least for a while.

Gary is very aware of the food he eats and its effect on his body – he finds that some foods affect him more than others. He told me:

> The main thing that makes me Phlegmy is milk – some grains do it as well and so does greasy food. Rice milk is OK and vegetables feel very good for me. When I eat foods which cause Phlegm I feel my throat constrict and my voice will get more tense. When I'm clear of Phlegm I feel lighter, my voice is clearer and it reverberates on my thorax which also feels clear.

If we need to stop eating certain foods it is always best to substitute healthier alternatives. For some suggestions see page 40.

Osteoporosis and dairy produce

Dairy produce in excess is Phlegm and Damp-forming for most of us. A number of people have said to me, 'If I cut down on dairy produce I'm worried that I'll succumb to osteoporosis or become very deficient in calcium.' This is not necessarily the case. The Chinese and Japanese have lived healthily on a diet containing little or no dairy produce for thousands of years. It is also ironic that the countries with the highest milk consumption (USA and Scandinavia) have the highest incidence of osteoporosis in the world.[13]

One of the best ways of preventing osteoporosis is regular weight-bearing exercise such as walking, running, cycling, swimming, playing racket games or dancing.[14] Chinese exercises such as Qigong or Tai Ji Quan can also be beneficial. More is written about these exercises in Chapter 4.

Dealing with Weight Problems

Many people in the West find it difficult to lose weight. In China, people who eat a traditional diet rarely have a weight problem as their diet nourishes the Stomach and Spleen.

The Stomach and Spleen are the two main organs of digestion and they are in charge of assimilating, moving and transforming our food and drink. Weight problems are often caused by eating food which weakens these two organs.

Losing Weight Effortlessly

Eat nourishing food but avoid dieting. A nourishing diet contains grains and beans with fresh vegetables and fruit. If these are taken in the correct proportions they will strengthen the Spleen and allow it to work at maximum capacity.

Eat three meals a day regularly. Skipping meals weakens the Spleen.

Cut down on Damp and Phlegm-forming food. These rich foods are sticky and difficult to digest and put a strain on the Spleen and Stomach (*see page 22*). Most people find that they effortlessly lose weight when they cut down or cut out wheat.

Avoid Cold foods and drink. This can be a major cause of weight problems. Cold slows movement down, while heat speeds it up. Taking foodstuffs such as iced drinks, frozen yogurts or too many raw vegetables will slow down the metabolism.

Avoid eating too much overly sweet food. The sweet taste is associated with the Spleen. A moderate amount of the sweet taste is very tonifying but an excess will weaken the Spleen. It is best to cut down on extremely sweet tasting food and best to avoid food sweetened with white sugar altogether.

Start doing moderate exercise. When we cut down on food the body thinks there is a famine and starts to conserve our food and energy. To lose weight we need to exercise, which will speed up the metabolism.

If we follow these and the rest of the dietary suggestions in this chapter, we will naturally reach a healthy equilibrium in our weight.

Meat-eating or Vegetarian – Which is the Healthy Choice?

There has been much discussion over the years about whether it is healthier to be a meat-eater or a vegetarian. Chinese medicine would say that we should only eat a small amount of meat because of its 'rich' qualities which we have already mentioned. Research bears out this view.

Too much meat

Too much meat can lead to a diet which is far too high in fat. Studies have been carried out in the West on the correlation between a regular high consumption of meat in the diet with coronary heart disease and many types of cancer.[15] Research carried out in the United States found a difference between people who consumed meat daily and those who didn't. Those who ate meat every day were found to have a 60 per cent greater chance of dying from coronary heart disease than those who consumed meat less than once a week.

Not enough meat

On the other hand, a lack of meat can lead to serious deficiency. A recent study has linked eating meat during pregnancy with healthier babies. In this study 549 women were surveyed between 1948 and 1954 and the offspring traced 40 years later. This research suggests that women who cut down on eating meat during pregnancy could risk producing children who suffer from an increased risk of high blood pressure and heart disease in middle age.[16]

Nourishing our 'Blood' by eating meat

The Chinese say that animal products such as meat and fish are especially effective for nourishing the 'Blood' in our bodies. They view Blood in a slightly different way from Western medicine. Chinese medicine teaches that Blood is responsible for 'nourishing and moistening' our systems and for keeping our 'spirit' settled in the body. Blood flows through vessels alongside our Qi energy. If we become 'Blood deficient' we can have symptoms such as anxiety, panics, insomnia and a poor memory. These are symptoms affecting our spirit. Other symptoms such as tiredness, cramps, pins and needles, light-headedness, dry skin, or floaters in front of the eyes can arise. This is because we are not properly nourished and moisturized by our Blood.

From these symptoms we can realize that Blood deficiency causes many disabling symptoms. These include anxiety, jumpiness and even a lack of confidence. A condition sometimes treated as a mental or emotional problem can simply be due to a deficient diet.

An 'almost' vegetarian diet

The Chinese recommend a compromise between vegetarianism and eating meat, in the form of an 'almost vegetarian diet'. We don't need to eat too much animal protein but a little will benefit our health. We only need to take 2–4 ounces of animal products 3–4 times a week. The Chinese often cut their meat, fish or poultry into small strips and mix it with their rice or noodles.

Sally's Indecision About Meat

Sally, who is 42 and a speech therapist, became convinced that she and her son needed meat in their diet. Both of them now feel the difference. Here she tells us what happened:

I went for acupuncture treatment as I had no reserves of energy left. With treatment I recovered my energy to a certain level but I always had to go back for more treatment every six weeks because my energy would crash down again. My practitioner said that my diet was the major factor stopping me from getting better. My husband and I had been vegetarian for 20 years and our children had never eaten meat. At first my practitioner's words didn't wash at all but I eventually changed my mind when my son Paul, who was coming up to 15 years, was also having problems.

At 15 he was under six stone, not tall and not going into puberty. He was also somewhat anorexic in his attitude to food. My practitioner said this might also be due to a lack of meat. Paul now eats meat 2–3 times a week with no comment and he's grown much taller and gone into puberty. He no longer looks as if he could be blown away by a puff of wind. Before he was having trouble getting through his studies, but now he's worked relatively hard for months without getting stressed at all.

I now eat meat too and it's made a huge difference – my tongue has actually changed color! It was always very pale, now it's a healthy red and I can hardly recognize it as mine.[17] I was always a wishy-washy person and as a child I was thought to be anemic, though blood tests showed that I wasn't. I now feel much stronger generally and feel fitter and I'm enjoying life more. I've even taken up tennis. In terms of treatment I now need much less. I went for a check-up in June then didn't go back until September and I was fine.

Dietary Tips for Vegetarians

Some people find it difficult to eat meat on moral grounds. If this is the case then it is important to eat a vegetarian diet which is as well-balanced as possible. Here are some guidelines for vegetarians:

DO'S AND DON'T'S FOR VEGETARIANS

Don't substitute meat with cheese or other dairy produce as this does not create a well-balanced diet – cheese and dairy products are extremely rich foods.

Try not to binge on sugary and fatty foods to make up for the lack of animal products and protein in the diet. The result of this can be huge shifts in mood and also weight gain.

To ensure eating adequate amounts of protein and 'Blood' nourishing foods vegetarians can:

Include plenty of grains in their diet and combine them with beans.[18]

Eat more protein substitutes. Two important ones come from soya beans. One is a product called 'tofu' and another is called 'miso', both are very nourishing.

Eat lots of seaweed products. Some common ones are hiziki, nori and wakame. Seaweed is commonly eaten in the Orient – more by the Japanese than the Chinese. It is very nourishing, low in fiber and also contains many minerals such as potassium, calcium, magnesium and iron as well as iodine (*see page 223 for cooking instructions*).

Eat sprouted beans – bean sprouts are considered to be energy enhancing foods (*see page 223*).

Eat plenty of dried fruits such as dates, apricots and figs to strengthen the Blood.

Eat lots of vegetables, especially leafy green vegetables.

Follow the suggestions in this book for balanced proportions in the diet.

How Anna Changed her Diet

Anna spoke at the beginning of this chapter about how she cured her irritable bowel syndrome by adjusting her diet. Here she tells us about the adjustments she made:

Before I changed my diet I never ate breakfast. I would also eat loads of peanuts. We had a peanut jar and I'd eat a couple of handfuls a day. For lunch I'd have a cheese dish like cheese on toast or a cheese sandwich and I'd have a glass of milk with it. In the evening I'd usually have a hot and spicy curry with lots of garlic and I'd ladle in loads of curry powder! During the day I'd drink loads of yogurt drinks, milkshakes and also iced fizzy drinks. I didn't eat any vegetables and had very little fruit.

My diet's not completely perfect yet but it's much better. I now eat porridge every morning for breakfast and make sure I have three meals a day with no snacks. At lunch I eat soup. I make sure it's not a creamy soup and it's usually made from vegetables – I love asparagus soup. With the soup I'll have a roll and butter and I'll also eat some fresh vegetables if I can. In the evening I no longer eat hot spicy food like I did. I'll usually eat something like a lasagne or another pasta dish and I'll have 2–3 vegetables with it and some fruit for pudding. I have meat 2–3 times a week, mainly white meat such as

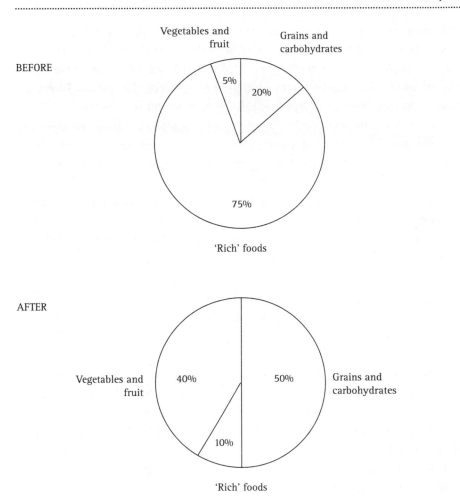

Figure 2: The proportions of Anna's diet before and after she changed it.

chicken or turkey, which I prefer. I never eat cheese, creamy things or peanuts now. I drink some tea or may often have some herb teas or water instead. I'll occasionally drink some alcohol but rarely.

By cutting out rich foods and substituting more fruit and vegetables, Anna has completely transformed her diet and consequently her health. The large proportion of 'rich' food was upsetting her bowels. Interestingly, both the iced drinks and the hot food were also exacerbating her bowel problem. More is written about 'heating' and 'cooling' foods on pages 34–57. Although as she says her diet is not 100 per cent perfect, the improvements are already having long-term repercussions on her overall well-being.

So far we have discussed making adjustments to the proportions of the food in our diets. Altering these proportions is often the first simple step towards making long lasting changes so that we become healthier in the future.

In Part 2 of this chapter we will find out about five other important areas of diet.

Part Two
Eating Healthily

Chinese medicine describes the digestive process as the 'rotting and ripening' of food and drink in the Stomach. This is followed by the 'transformation and transportation' of food carried out by the other digestive organs. If we take in good quality food it will be transformed into high quality Qi and Blood. This nourishes us on all levels – physically, mentally and spiritually. The result is that we can begin to glow with good health.

If we eat low quality food it lowers our vitality – the quality of our Qi and Blood will be poor. Over time this will result in ill-health. To ensure that we create the best possible quality of Qi and Blood from our diet, we will now consider five other important areas.

1 Eating good quality food.
2 Enjoying our food.
3 The temperature of food.
4 The taste of food.
5 Eating in the right conditions.

We will start by considering the quality of our food. This includes the purity and freshness of our diet.

Eating Good Quality Food

Hormones and antibiotics injected into animals, pesticides sprayed on vegetables, preservatives in food and pollution in the air. More recently, genetically modified foods have been introduced into the food chain. These must all be having a profound effect on our long-term health. Unless we are eating organic foods we are now eating these pesticides, preservatives and drugs on a daily basis. Many of us are becoming increasingly aware that the human race cannot disturb nature without detrimental effects.

The BSE crisis in Great Britain is one example of the damage caused by interfering with nature. Other effects from long-term use of chemicals are bound to become more apparent in the years to come. Problems arising from tampering with our foodstuffs are relatively new and are not of course mentioned in old Chinese texts. The best advice for us to follow is to eat simple, natural foodstuffs which are in season and grown around us if possible. These are the foods that our ancestors ate on a daily basis.

Organic foods

Nowadays the most unadulterated foods are ones we carefully grow in our own gardens or organically grown food. All food should be processed as little as possible. Organic vegetables, fruit and meat products are now widely available and many of us are eating them as a part of our daily diet. They have the added advantage of tasting better as well as being healthier. Organic meat may be a more expensive option but the cost can be made up by eating smaller amounts.

If I can't buy organic what can I eat?

Vegetables which are not organic have usually been treated with pesticides. There are over 100 types of pesticides, including many organophosphates, on the market. These can permeate the roots of vegetables and can't be removed just by rinsing. Pesticides are known to be extremely toxic and have been linked to low sperm counts and cancer.[19] Research by the Soil Association and others in Britain has shown that many vegetables on the market contain pesticides above the official safety levels. Francis Blake, Director of Certification at the Soil Association explains:[20]

> Carrots are the main root vegetable affected by organophosphates. The carrot root fly is difficult to treat and damage to the carrot makes it unsalable. For this reason farmers use insecticides in the soil. Swedes can also be affected. The least affected root vegetables are beetroots, parsnips and celeriac although none are totally clear of pesticides.
>
> Leafy vegetables are better than root vegetables but consumers should be aware that nitrites in the soil will concentrate at the heart of leafy vegetables so it is better to eat the outside leaves of non-organic vegetables. These also contain the most vitamins and minerals.

For those who can't afford organic vegetables or are eating out we can at least take Francis Blake's advice and take care of what we eat. Likewise, eating fish dishes may be the safest alternative for many people who enjoy going out to eat – the seas are polluted but at least the fish haven't been injected with hormones! Sally, who talked about bringing meat into her diet (*see page 26*), still doesn't eat meat when she goes out. She told me:

> I only eat organic meat now. We eat meat at home as a family but to everyone else we are vegetarians. I now really enjoy meats like organic lamb – I wouldn't have eaten the ordinary stuff before as it had no taste.

Eating Fresh Foods which are not 'Spoiled'

The Chinese call food which is no longer fresh 'Spoiled' food. Cooked food that is more than 24 hours old loses some of its vitamins and minerals but more importantly it begins to also lose its Qi content. We already mentioned that Chinese medicine teaches us that if we eat well we gain Qi from our food. Over recent years the West has created another kind of 'Spoiled food' which was unknown to the ancient Chinese. This is food which has very little

Qi content due to irradiation, preservatives and other added chemicals and also by using cooking methods such as microwaving.

Food rotted and ripened in the Stomach is called 'Grain Qi'. This Grain Qi mixes with the air we breathe and is refined until it becomes our 'True Qi'. Chinese medicine teaches that the Spleen moves and transforms our Qi and Body Fluids. This carries True Qi all over the body allowing it to nourish our whole system. If our Qi is strong we can ward off infections and have good vitality. We can also have that feeling of 'being happy to be alive' that we referred to on page 12.

In order to enhance our Qi it is best to eat food which is as fresh, pure and alive as possible. A useful rule of thumb when choosing food to eat is, 'If it can't go off don't eat it. If it can go off only eat it when it's fresh.'

Enjoying our Food

The second significant factor in our diet is enjoying our food. If we smell a really tasty dish cooking in the kitchen it activates our salivary glands and we start to feel hungry. Our saliva then breaks down the food we put in our mouth. When the food reaches the Stomach it can be 'rotted and ripened' more easily and we then get more Qi and nourishment from it. If we don't enjoy our food we won't salivate and we won't digest it properly.

If we enjoy our new diet it will be easy for us to include nourishing foods in our meals. But what if we find it hard to build up an appetite for the food we are eating? Too rich a diet such as chips, burgers and ice cream can become addictive. A diet high in vegetables and grains can at first seem extremely boring in comparison. A rich diet can be hard to give up yet we can get caught in the trap of feeling guilty if we don't stick to our new healthier routine. Guilt is as harmful as a poor diet.

Sometimes the only food available to us is not particularly healthy or nourishing. For example, we're away from home or work at lunch time and can only find a burger bar. If this is the case we can decide to eat with relish and *as if* it is nourishing – at least our mental state will then be positive and help us to gain the best possible nourishment from it.

Tips to make food enjoyable

Many of the people I spoke to had ingenious ways of making their diet more enjoyable. For instance James told me:

> I knew I needed to change my diet to become healthier but at first my old diet seemed more exciting than other foods. I allowed myself a treat of one 'old style' meal per fortnight. After a few weeks the pasta, rice and vegetables seemed to be tastier than what I had eaten before. I do still allow myself treats every so often. Knowing that I can have an occasional coffee or chips makes it easier.

Eileen found out that we eat with our minds as much as with our bodies:

> Making my food look attractive was the way I tempted myself to eat better. I really enjoyed making my food look nice. I was also strongly motivated to eat well as I knew it would be better for my health.

Tony found regularity to be important too:

> I began to get hungry when I started to eat regular meals. Three to four weeks after I started to eat that way I found I was hungry at every meal. It kind of clicked into place.

Whichever way we choose, it is important to make our diet enjoyable as well as healthy. If we are eating a diet which is not appetizing we won't stick with it. Remember that it takes a month to really alter our habits. Once we have made the adjustments for a month they will seem natural and more easily integrated into our daily lives.

The Temperature of Food

The third important aspect to do with our diet is choosing food at a correct temperature and taste. These are secrets which have been well kept from the West. We'll start by looking at the fascinating area of temperature.

Chinese medicine understands that some foods are colder in their nature and that others are warmer. This is not dependent on whether the food has been warmed up or frozen but is rather something about its inherent nature. Food is divided into Hot, Warm, Neutral, Cool and Cold.

Below is a list of some foods and their temperatures:[21]

Hot, Warm, Neutral, Cool and Cold Foods

Hot Black pepper, butter, chicken fat, chocolate, coffee, crispy rice, curry, hot chilies, lamb, onions, peanut butter, sesame seeds, smoked fish, trout, whisky.

Warm Barley, beef, black-eyed beans, brown sugar, cheese, chestnut, chicken meat, egg yolk, dates, garlic, ginger, green (bell) pepper, ham, kidney beans, leeks, lobster, mussels, oats, peach, pomegranate, potato, prawns, shrimps, turkey, turnip, walnuts, vinegar, wine.

Neutral Adzuki beans, apricots, beetroot, black tea, bread, broad beans, brown rice, cabbage, carrots, cherries, corn, egg white, chickpeas (garbanzos), grapes, honey, hot water, lentils, kidney beans, milk, oysters, peanuts, peas, plum, pork, raisins, red beans, rye, salmon, sugar, sweet potatoes.

Cool Almonds, apples, asparagus, barley, broccoli, cabbage, cauliflower, celery, chicory, corn, fish, mushrooms, mango, mung beans, oranges, pears, pineapple, radishes, rhubarb, salt, seaweed, soya beans, spinach, strawberry, tangerines, turnip, wheat, wild rice.

Cold Banana, bean sprouts, cucumber, duck, grapefruit, green tea, lettuce, ice cream, peppermint, sorbet, tofu, tomato, water melon, yogurt.

You will find a questionnaire on page 206. Some of the questions will help you to discover whether you are more Hot or Cold. You might then bias your diet towards eating slightly more heating or cooling foods. It is best to choose from the Neutral foods for the largest percentage of our diet. Ones from the Cool or Warm section should be taken in slightly lesser quantities. Foods that are very Hot or very Cold only need to be taken in small amounts as they are too extreme to be taken in large quantities and may cool us down or heat us up too much. Fruit is a good example.

Cooling and Cold foods

Not surprisingly many fruits which are cooling in their nature grow in a more tropical climate. Fruits such as tangerines, oranges, pineapples, bananas, melons and grapefruit are pleasant treats especially in hot weather when they will cool us down. They should not, however, be taken in large quantities in cold weather.

Too much Cold food can give us symptoms such as loose bowels, profuse urination, stomach aches or period pains. Over a long period they could also make us feel tired inside through weakening the Stomach and Spleen.

Some people think that large quantities of fruit juice such as orange juice is good for them. Drinking even one glass of fruit juice is similar to eating 8–10 oranges at once and can be extremely rich as well as Cold. As with other foods, we should bear in mind whether food is in season and where it is grown. Locally grown food which is in season is always our best choice.

Warm and Heating foods

You might also notice that many meats and fatty foods such as butter, chicken fat, lamb, beef and peanuts are more Heating in nature. We know that these are nourishing in small quantities but they should not be taken in large amounts.

Large amounts of Heating foods can make us restless, irritable and angry and could give us symptoms such as high blood pressure, headaches, palpitations or constipation.

Balancing Hot and Cold foods

If we do eat Hot foods we can balance them by picking a food from the Cooler section and vice versa. For example, tofu and other soya products are quite Cooling in nature. Adding a little ginger, which is a Heating food, can make them more warming. Lamb which is very Hot is traditionally combined with mint sauce to Cool it down.

Rice is one of the best grains that we can eat. It has a Neutral temperature so can be eaten in large quantities and it also clears Dampness from our system.

The Taste of Food

A variety of tastes in our diets keeps it balanced and our food interesting. Chinese medicine divides the tastes into five different categories which are Bitter, Sweet, Pungent, Salty and Sour. These affect the functioning of the corresponding organ shown in the list below.[22]

Flavors of Foods and Their Associated Organs

Bitter (Heart and Small Intestine)
Alfalfa, asparagus, beer, broccoli, celery, chicory, coffee, grapefruit rind, lettuce, radish, raspberry leaf tea, turnip, vinegar, watercress.

Sweet (Stomach and Spleen)
Adzuki beans, apple, apricot, barley, beef, beetroots cabbage, carrot, celery, cheese, cherry, chicken, chickpeas, coffee, courgette (zucchini), corn, cucumber, dates, grapes, grapefruit, honey, kidney beans, lamb, lettuce, malt, mandarin, mung beans, mushroom, orange, milk, oats, peach, peanuts, pear, pineapple, plum, pork, potato, radish, raspberry, rice, spinach, strawberry, sugar, tomato, walnut, wheat, wine.

Pungent (Lung and Large Intestine)
Black pepper, cayenne pepper, cabbage, cherry, chili, cloves, cumin, garlic, green (bell) pepper, horseradish, leek, marjoram, mint, mustard, nutmeg, peppermint, radish, rosemary, soya oil, turnip, watercress, wheat germ, wine.

Salty (Kidney and Bladder)
Barley, crab, duck, garlic, ham, kelp, lobster, millet, mussel, oyster, pork, salt, sardine, seaweed.

> **Sour (Liver and Gall Bladder)**
> Adzuki beans, apples, apricot, blackberry, blackcurrant, cheese, crabapple,
> gooseberry, grape, grapefruit, green leafy vegetables, lemons, lychee,
> mandarin orange, mango, olive, peach, pear, pineapple, plum,
> pomegranate, raspberry, sour plums, strawberry, tomato, trout,
> tangerine, vinegar.

Each of these different tastes will affect us in different ways and all food has one or a combination of these tastes. You may notice, for example, that a radish is both Bitter and Sweet, whilst garlic is Salty and Pungent. We'll briefly talk about each of these tastes in turn.

Bitter

Bitter foods slightly cool the body and are used to stimulate the digestion. They can also be used to cool fevers and to clear bowel problems which are due to heat. They should only be used in small quantities in our diet if Qi is deficient, because of their purging action.

Sweet

The Sweet flavor described in Chinese medicine is a subtle flavor. It is different from the strong sugary taste of sweet that is often used in the West. Sweet is probably one of the most frequent tastes found in foods – note the number of sweet foods listed in the category above. The sweet taste affects the Stomach and Spleen. In Chinese medicine these organs have the function of transforming all of our food and drink in order to nourish us. If taken in the correct quantities, Sweet foods such as rice, chicken, cabbage and carrots will have a tonifying effect.

Extremely sweet foods in large quantities will weaken the Stomach and Spleen and have a Dampening effect. People frequently crave chocolates and sweets because their Stomach and Spleen are deficient. This can become a vicious cycle and the more depleted these organs become the more we crave sweet foods. The Stomach and Spleen then correspondingly become even more feeble. This will result in very deficient Qi in our whole system or even malnutrition.

Pungent

Pungent foods are sharp and acrid in their taste and include common foods such as garlic, ginger, chili pepper and cinnamon. The effect of large amounts of the pungent taste is to disperse and move obstructions in the Qi and Blood. Like Bitter, they should be taken in small quantities by anyone who has very deficient energy.

Salty

The Salty flavor is commonly found in seaweed and seafood such as sardines, crab, lobster and mussels. The salty taste acts as a diuretic and will clear excess water from the system. People are advised frequently to avoid salt in their diet and it is true that it is best not to take an excessive amount. This is especially the case if a person retains fluids and has weak Kidneys which are the organs associated with this taste. A small amount of salt can be beneficial, however, if a person is too dry as it will encourage moisture in the body.

Sour

Finally Sour foods have the opposite effect to Pungent ones. They stop discharges and are astringent in their action. They help problems such as urinary incontinence, diarrhea or excessive sweating.

Balancing temperature and tastes

Chinese cuisine at its most excellent will demonstrate how to combine Warm, Neutral and Cool foods as well as including a good balance of all of the tastes.

In general it is best to include all the flavors in our diet without eating any of them in excessive amounts or as too strong a taste. If we crave a certain taste this may indicate that the associated organ is out of balance. A small amount of a food may enhance the functioning of that organ. Greater quantities make an imbalance more extreme.

Substitutes for Some Common Foods

If you need to give up or reduce your intake of certain foods it is always best to substitute with an alternative. Here are some suggestions:

Dairy products
Replace with soya milk – try different ones as some taste better than others. Alternatively use rice or oat milk.
Use small amounts of sheep's or goat's cheese, yogurt or milk.

Orange juice
Dilute apple, pear or grape juice concentrate.
Drink mineral water.

Coffee and tea
Herb teas.
Coffee substitutes such as 'Caro' or 'Barleycup'.
Rooibosch (redbush) tea which is low in caffeine and tannin.

Hot spices
Use milder herbs for flavoring.
Smaller amounts of spices.
Soya sauce.

Sugary foods
Use foods with a natural sweetness such as sweet potatoes, parsnips, carrots or peas (not frozen with added sugar!).
Find foods which have been naturally sweetened with apple juice or molasses.
Avoid artificial sweeteners.
Carob is a useful substitute for chocolate (an acquired taste if you're a chocoholic!).

Fatty red meat
Eat organic meat – remove the fat.
Take more fish (oily fish is best) and poultry.
Eat tofu burgers, sausages and bean and lentil dishes.

Alcohol

Drink occasional low alcohol lager.

Occasional organic wine or beer.[23]

Wheat

Eat rice, oats, rye and products made from other grains (*see page 220 for cooking grains*).

Eat fresh rye bread or rye bread in the form of pumpernickel bread.

Use wheat free pasta and other products (the Terence Stamp range is very good).

Eat oat biscuits or rice cakes.

Find wheat free 'bars' for a healthy snack – usually available in health food shops.

Eating in the Right Conditions

The fifth important aspect of diet is eating regularly and in the correct conditions. The importance of this cannot be overemphasized in relation to our diet.

Eating regularly

The Stomach likes regularity. When we eat regularly, we start to feel hungry at those times as we mentally and physically prepare to eat. Here is Jack's comment about eating regularly:

I used to be a real picker. One day I'd pig out then the next day I didn't eat. If I pigged out it affected my energy and the next day I often felt muzzy in my head. Now I eat three meals a day and I don't need to eat in between. The result is that my energy is spaced out more evenly during the day.

Creating a routine will stabilize our dietary habits. This means that we are less likely to eat convenience foods and will eat in a way which is good for our health and well-being. We also need to consider the times when we eat during the day. Anita told me:

> At one time although I usually had breakfast and lunch, in the evening
> I would eat at any old time, often quite late and usually with loads of meat –
> I think I believed my stomach was indestructible! Then I became diabetic and
> had to change. I began to eat regularly and started to take my evening meal
> at 6pm. I also controlled my carbohydrate levels and reduced my protein
> intake. Although I was diabetic I felt healthier for eating regularly.

Avoiding eating late at night

If we eat late at night our body will not have enough time to digest our food before we go to sleep. Our sleep should nourish us. If we are still digesting food at night, less energy will be available to replenish us and we may wake up feeling tired. Continually eating late can lead to insomnia or light sleeping. It can also contribute to even more serious illnesses such as diabetes.

Allowing time for digestion

As well as eating regularly, we can also strive to eat in conditions which assist our Stomach and Spleen to assimilate our food. Nowadays many people don't find the time to sit down and properly digest their food. Compare this to the Chinese.

The Chinese typically take their lunch and then relax and maybe even cat-nap for half an hour afterwards. The rest will allow them to digest their food and prepare for their afternoon activities. This strategy means that they feel ready to accomplish their tasks twice as efficiently as those who have not taken a break.

Many of us may remember that our grandparents also took this time to relax. Here a friend talks about her granddad:

> I remember staying with my granddad on his farm. After lunch, without fail,
> he'd have half-an-hour's rest. He'd then wake up looking completely
> refreshed and go back to work again. He was a very sturdy man and I'm sure
> it must have enabled him to continue the work he did well into old age.

It is now common for people to eat on the run and take a very short lunch-break instead of sitting down to eat properly. Often people take their meals while they are stressed or involved in other situations such as watching television, reading a book, sitting at their computer or making business deals. Here are some useful ways that will help us to digest our food properly in order to gain more energy from it:

Gaining Energy from our Food

Eat only until you're 70 per cent full

Eating until you are full up and bloated will strain the Qi of your Stomach and Spleen. As the famous Chinese text Simple Questions states: 'Overeating impairs the Intestines and the Stomach.' (*See page 90 for more on the 70 per cent rule and exercise.*)

Don't eat a meal while you're still digesting a previous meal

This can lead to the contents of your Stomach stagnating and can cause indigestion.

Eat three meals a day including breakfast

If you skip breakfast your energy level may drop later in the morning. This can cause cravings for chocolate or other sugary snacks. Remember the saying 'Eat like a king for breakfast, a prince for lunch and a pauper for supper.'

Chew your food well

This helps the digestive juices to break down your food. It's also better to talk between mouthfuls rather than while you are actually chewing your food.

Drink most of your fluids between meals

Chinese people tend to sip green tea. Drinking vast amounts with your food will tend to flood the Spleen and give it more work to do. In general try to avoid caffeinated drinks like tea and coffee and colas as they are overstimulating. Warm water is best or simple herb teas.

Always sit down to eat and allow some time to digest your meal properly
Preferably find somewhere to eat lunch away from your normal workspace.
Don't eat on the run.
Take a short rest after eating lunch. This should be no more than half an
hour but will prepare you for the afternoon's activities.

Eat in a calm environment
If possible, it is better not to eat while you're angry or unhappy as it is more
difficult to digest food in these circumstances. It is also not a good idea
to eat while watching television, reading, discussing emotional issues or
doing anything that takes your mind away from your food.

Avoid eating too much Cold food
The body needs heat in order to digest food. Cold food slows down our
metabolism.

Becoming Sensitive to our Dietary Needs

If we relax and 'listen' to our bodies we will become increasingly aware of
which foods enhance our health and which make us less healthy. There are a
number of ways which might help us to notice how we are reacting.

Listening to our bodies

Firstly, if we tune into our bodies for a few minutes after eating we might
notice that we have certain responses which let us know that our body is
sensitive to a particular food. Common responses are:

- Bloating up after eating
- A feeling of Phlegm arising in the throat or chest
- Headaches
- Indigestion
- Belching and wind
- Discomfort in the Stomach area

- General lethargy
- Heaviness

These are only a few of many possible responses – it can be important to spend time noticing the different effects of certain foods. Earlier Gary spoke about the effects of Phlegm forming foods on his throat. He later said:

> I've found it useful to compare how I feel after days of eating badly and then eating well. After I eat lots of vegetables for a number of days I feel much better. If I eat more dairy products or greasy food I feel less well.

Food cravings

Secondly, any extreme craving or dislike of a food may indicate that we are sensitive to it. It's ironic that the foods we crave are often the ones which are having the most negative effect on our health. If we notice we're craving a specific food it may initially take a great deal of motivation to eliminate that food from our diet. It's probably best to decide to stop eating the 'offending' food for only a few weeks and to see what difference it makes to our health. If we then feel better we may be motivated to cut it out completely. It won't be long before the craving disappears and is replaced with a feeling of relief that we've eliminated a food which is not beneficial to our health.

'Suspect' food

Finally, sometimes we don't have cravings or responses to eating certain foods but still wonder if our symptoms are due to our diet. After reading this chapter, for example, we might decide we need less Phlegm and Damp-forming foods or need to add more vegetables or meat to our diets. In this case making the alteration and then noticing how our health changes over a period of three or four weeks will signal if the change has been a positive one.

Remember, foods come in groups, for example, dairy produce covers a wide range of foods as does wheat and there are a large number of foods with eggs or sugar in them.

We mentioned earlier how important it is to substitute foods when changing our diets (*see page 40*). It can be useful to prepare in advance when planning to eliminate foods from our diet and find tasty substitutes beforehand. There is a wide variety available in the supermarkets and health food shops. If we don't substitute we will make it far more difficult to make the changes we require. If we search out substitutes we enjoy, the adjustments become easy.

We've now covered all the secrets of a balanced diet. The two parts of this chapter aim to give you flexible guidelines which will enable you to develop good dietary habits. You can adapt this health-maintaining diet to suit your individual needs. Before we end this chapter here are examples of typical diets eaten by three people – Simon, Indira and Hannah, with some suggested changes they could introduce to improve their health.

Simon's Diet

Simon is 35 and enjoys his job as a sales rep because he drives all over the country. He is becoming increasingly concerned about his headaches as well as complaining of feeling lethargic and tired much of the time. He sleeps well but often is so tired he finds it hard to get up in the morning. The headaches come on every three or four days and are located on his forehead. They make his head feel heavy and are often worse after lunch. Sometimes when he is stressed the headache is all over his head and he feels as if his head will burst. This is the food he eats on a normal day:

8.00 Breakfast: A bowl of cereal with plenty of full cream milk and sugar. A cup of coffee.

11.00 Break at a cafe: Cup of coffee and cake.

1.00 Lunch: A good fry-up at a motorway cafe – sausage, egg and chips. Apple pie and also a cup of coffee.

3.30 Break: Cup of coffee and a cream cake.

5.00 Stop on way home: Cup of coffee.

9.00 Evening meal: After arriving home at 7.00. Pasta with a creamy sauce and vegetables with a piece of fruit. Cup of tea.

Simon's dietary problems

Simon's main problems are his high fat and dairy intake and too much coffee. The fatty food and dairy produce has put a strain on his Stomach, Spleen and Liver and have caused him to form Damp in his system. The Damp has caused him to feel heavy and lethargic. The Damp is also causing the headaches. The coffee will irritate the Stomach and Liver and make his headache worse. He is eating late at night which will strain his Stomach which will be digesting food late. He is getting some fruit and vegetables but not enough. It won't be easy for him to always eat well but he can look for the healthiest alternatives. His stressful lifestyle driving to different parts of the country is also contributing to his health problems.

Suggestions for Simon

Cut down on fat: Change to soya milk on cereal or have porridge. Choose less fatty options to eat at meals out if possible – there are usually some low fat meals available. Have non-creamy sauces on the pasta or other dishes eaten in the evening.

Cut down on coffee: Change to coffee substitutes when at home, taking alternative hot drinks in a flask or drinking mineral water at room temperature.

Eat as wholesome a diet as possible: Try to eat more fresh vegetables and fruit when out at lunch. Many restaurants will sell them. Eat other grains such as rice in the evening.

Arrange to eat earlier in the evening: Simon and his wife share the cooking. He can arrange to cook on the days he can get home earlier.

Do some gentle exercise in the morning or during the day: Simon is leading a very static life and needs more exercise. Some Qigong in the morning will get his energy moving before he drives off for the day.

Indira's Diet

Indira is 54 and is married with grown-up children. She came to England from India six years ago and feels settled in London where she lives. She works in her husband's shop during the day. Recently she has become worried about her health. Her doctor has told her that her blood pressure is getting quite high and she has also been getting indigestion and heartburn quite severely. This is what Indira eats on a normal day:

8.00 Breakfast: Spicy parathas which are made from special wheat flour and stuffed with potatoes.

12.30 Lunch: Spicy dahl (which is made from lentils) with rice and cooked vegetables.

6.00 Supper: Plain chapatis with spicy chicken curry, rice and vegetables. Milk pudding. A glass of water.

Between meals she may drink plain water or a special Indian brew of tea.

Indira's dietary problems

The spicy food in Indira's diet is causing most of her problems. When she was in India this spicy food was a necessary part of the diet – the chili peppers made her perspire and cooled her down in the strong heat. Now in England she is still eating the same diet but the climate is cold and damp and she doesn't perspire. The spicy food is staying in her system and is causing her Stomach and Liver to overheat. The Heat is causing her blood pressure to rise and is also irritating her Stomach.

Suggestions for Indira

Cut down on the spicy food: Indira uses large quantities of chili powder in each meal. She is advised to cut it by half.

Cut down on salt: She uses a lot of salt in her cooking and this is putting a strain on her system, causing her blood pressure to rise.

Use less grease in cooking: A lot of the ingredients of the dahl are cooked in oil and the vegetables are stir-fried.

Indira's basic diet is good. She eats at regular times and has a large amount of grains, beans and vegetables.

Hannah's Diet

Hannah is 19 and works in an office from 9.00–5.00. She has problems with her weight and finds it fluctuates a lot. She has recently started bloating after her meals. She also finds she gets spots on her face, especially before her period and she is also often constipated. This is what she eats on a normal day:

8.00   Cup of coffee. Leaves for work having skipped breakfast.

10.00   Chocolate bar.

1.00   Sandwich – either cheese or egg salad, a packet of crisps and an apple.

3.00   Biscuit.

5.00   Leaves work. May have a chocolate biscuit or two when she gets home.

6.30   Evening meal. Heat up a precooked meal from the supermarket with vegetables.

Coffee and tea throughout the day sweetened with an artificial sweetener.

Hannah's dietary problems

Hannah's main problem is a weak Spleen. The Spleen is responsible for transporting food and drink in the body. Her current diet is not nourishing her Spleen and she is eating excessively sweet tasting food which is further weakening her Spleen. The Spleen deficiency is making her bloat, is causing her intestines to become sluggish and is giving her spots.

Suggestions for Hannah

Hannah is advised to add more nourishing food to her diet.

Take the time to eat a nourishing breakfast: She may have to get up slightly earlier to do this but a warming bowl of porridge will set her up for the day. Her blood sugar has probably been dropping in the mid-morning causing her to crave chocolate and a good breakfast will stop this happening.

49

Substitute healthier snacks: If she finds it difficult to cut out the chocolate she can do it gradually. Carob can substitute for chocolate until she looses the addiction or snacks sweetened with apple juice or molasses.

Eat a hot meal at lunchtime: Take a hot nourishing soup – a vegetable soup made the night before – will fill her up. This can be eaten with a wholemeal roll or rice cakes.

Eat more fruit, vegetables and grains: She could put fruit on her porridge. She already gets vegetables in the evening and this is good. Avoiding the precooked meals and making rice dishes or wholemeal pasta would be a healthier choice for the evening.

Substitute alternative drinks to tea and coffee: Artificial sweeteners will encourage her taste for sweet food. Occasional tea and coffee is fine but she needs to drink far less of it. She can start with naturally decaffeinated tea such as Rooibosh and coffee substitutes instead.

These are a lot of changes for Hannah to make so she might choose to do them gradually. She could start with the porridge, hot soup and healthy evening meal. As she notices the difference to her health she might feel inspired to make more changes.

At the end of this book is a questionnaire (*see page 212*). Many parts of it will answer questions about your specific dietary needs. If you are ill it is always best to get the advice of a doctor or a practitioner of Chinese medicine rather than trying to cure yourself by diet alone.

Summary

1 Eat a diet of the correct proportions with lots of grains and vegetables and cut down on rich foods such as dairy produce, animal products, fats and sweets. Eat vegetables cooked rather than raw, avoid Phlegm and Damp-forming foods and eat an 'almost' vegetarian diet. A well balanced diet will allow you to lose weight effortlessly.

2 Eat good quality food – organic is best. Old food is called 'Spoiled' food by the Chinese and contains less Qi.

3 Enjoy your food. Make it as pleasant tasting and smelling as possible. If you have to give yourself a few 'treats', it is better than feeling guilt-ridden about eating badly.

4 Balance the 'temperature' of foods.

5 Have a variety of tastes in your diet.

6 Eat regularly and in the right conditions – give yourself space to eat and give yourself time to digest your food.

The Secret of Balancing Our Emotions

Part One
Emotions as a Cause of Disease

Two well-known and much quoted Chinese proverbs state that 'A person should laugh three times a day to live longer,' and 'A good laugh makes you 10 years younger, whilst worry turns the hair gray.'

We may once have regarded these as light-hearted sayings. Research has shown that this is not the case. Laughing and keeping positive really are the secrets of good health.

A research project carried out at the State University of New York found that laughter increased the levels of an antibody called 'immunoglobulin A' which is found in the lining of the nose. This antibody helps people to fight illnesses. People with fewer antibodies were more prone to colds and other infections. The researchers asked 72 men to fill in a form every evening for 12 weeks describing how their day had been. Each man also kept a mucous sample which was analyzed for antibody levels. The research found that the level of antibodies was higher on the days where the men had laughed a lot or good things had happened, whilst on bad days the antibody level was lower.[1]

Other research has found that people who are optimistic are likely to be healthier later on in their life than those who are pessimistic. One study began in the 1940s. Ninety-nine healthy and successful graduates from Harvard University filled out questionnaires which determined their level of optimism or pessimism. They then completed questionnaires each year and were examined by a physician every five years until the age of 60.

Although all graduates were healthy when they left Harvard, the results showed that pessimism in early adulthood is a risk factor for ill-health in middle and late adulthood. By the age of 60, 13 of these people had died. Those who were more optimistic remained in better health and were at their healthiest between 40 and 45. Stunningly, there was a less than 1 in 1,000 chance that these results were random – not even the statistical link between lung cancer and smoking is as strong as that![2]

If laughter and optimism have positive effects on our health, what are the effects of negative emotions?

The Internal Causes of Disease

Anger, Fear, Joy, Grief, Shock, Worry and Sadness are all emotions which the Chinese recognize can affect our health. The Chinese named these emotions the 'Internal causes' of disease because we generate them from inside ourselves. In contrast, illnesses caused by weather conditions like Heat, Cold or Damp are called 'External causes'. 'Lifestyle causes' such as diet, exercise or overwork are called 'not Internal and not External causes'.

Although the Chinese named only seven emotions as Internal causes, these seven include all other emotions. For example, frustration, depression, resentment, irritation, bitterness and rage all come under the general heading of Anger. Fear can also be fright, terror or anxiety. Grief can include emptiness, longing, regret or remorse.

In this chapter we will be looking at the effects of these emotions on our health and discuss some ways of dealing with them.

Emotions as a Cause of Disease

It is natural for us to experience a variety of emotions when different circumstances occur in our lives. Fear protects us from danger, Anger helps

us to assert our rights and it is normal to feel Grief when we have lost someone or something.

How our emotions can cause illness

All emotions are normal in the appropriate circumstances and we usually
recover from their effects. But what happens when we have a sustained emotion over a long period of time? Here Paul describes the devastating effects
the break-up of his marriage had on his health.

> I've noticed that since the trauma of my marriage break-up my face has
> deteriorated around my eyes. My whole body also deteriorated – my bowels
> became irregular and I had discomfort in my chest and stomach all the time.
> It felt worse than a bereavement – I couldn't accept that after 22 years we
> had broken up.

Emotions tend to cause disease when they are extremely prolonged or intense, or if they are not expressed or acknowledged.

Emotional traumas often start when we are children, a time when we have
no means of protecting ourselves. As children we rely on our parents to love,
protect and nurture us, as well as to show us right from wrong and teach us
boundaries. Most of us don't have a perfect childhood but what devastates
one child may have little or no effect on another. Children may have been
disturbed by a variety of events such as being bullied at school, being scared
of exams, moving home, losing friends or parents quarrelling.

If the emotional effects of life's circumstances are not dealt with, the scars
can stay with the child and manifest later in life as ill-health. Children who
are under five at the time of a family break-up are up to five times more
likely to have a psychiatric illness later on in life.

Let's take a further look at the emotional causes of disease and how they
affect us.

Anger

Much research has been carried out on the effects of Anger on our health. One study conducted at universities in Miami and California involved 27 people, two-thirds of whom were suffering from heart disease and one-third of whom were not. The subjects were tested while they were exercising and also while undergoing other psychological stressors. The psychological stressors included making a speech, doing mental arithmetic and recalling an event which made them angry. The study found that everyone's heart was more affected by situations that made them angry than by exercise or any of the other psychological stressors.[3]

Pressure at work can also cause Anger and frustration. Sue describes how this affected her:

> I'd always worked in high pressure jobs and often in personnel. It was very frustrating as I was trying to help people but I couldn't. Instead, I was doing things like making people redundant. Seeing people suffering was so frustrating and I kept the feelings inside. I had bad PMT, mood swings and in the end I got a benign tumor on my spine. That was the real warning sign that I needed to change.

Here Charles describes how long-term frustration and Anger affected his health.

> I drove a lorry for five years. It was hard work and I never got any thanks. People there expressed very little emotion about things but everyone showed a lot of bravado. Over the five years I became increasingly frustrated and angered by their attitude but I never expressed how I felt. Over time I found I became more and more tired and depressed. I also got a very stiff neck and photophobia – the inability to take bright lights – I couldn't even go into a house with white walls as they were too bright. I was much better after I left the job and became self-employed.

Chinese medicine teaches us that the organs have other 'functions' beyond the characteristics defined by Western medicine. Different emotions affect these functions in the different organs. Anger will affect the functions connected to the Liver. Interestingly, one Liver function is to allow the Qi to flow smoothly and easily throughout the body. If the Qi flow is smooth, then we are relaxed. When we are angry or tense the Qi can become constricted. Many of the symptoms of PMT (which Sue experienced) are due to this lack of free flowing Qi. Other symptoms include tension, bloating, swollen breasts and mood swings. The Liver also affects the eyes and influences the eyesight, which explains why Charles developed photophobia.

It is disturbing to note that many of us like Sue and Charles are finding our living circumstances are having a negative effect on our health. In consumer research carried out by the National Opinion Poll, it was found that 90 per cent of people said they now flare up more than they did 10 years ago and 10 per cent of people said they lose their temper more than once a day. Being kept on hold on the phone was considered the most stressful situation, closely followed by road rage.[4]

The increasing pace of life results in more tension. As people become more pressured we need to find better ways of dealing with the diseases which ensue. Treating only the symptoms of stress is not enough. Chinese medicine and all holistic therapies teach that dealing with the underlying cause is the only way in which ill-health can truly be tackled. Unexpressed Anger is probably one of the most common causes of ill-health in modern day society. Later we will look at some ways that will help us to deal with our Anger as well as other emotions (*see page 61*).

Other common and potentially disruptive emotions are Fear, anxiety and Worry.

Fear, Anxiety and Worry

We feel angry in response to something that has upset us in the past or present. In contrast, Fear, anxiety and Worry are felt about what the future holds in store for us. Often the events we anticipate don't materialize – knowing that we have wasted time feeling highly stressed for no good reason doesn't, however, help a persistent worrier to stop. Worry and anxiety often affect the Stomach and other digestive functions, as Sandra discovered. She told me:

> I feel Worry has a direct effect on my health. It may be only slight Worry but it all goes straight to my guts. If I've got to get a lot done my guts will tighten up. When I'm not worried I'll be calm and settled and my health is much better.

Research carried out at Yale University substantiates this. Two researchers synthesized studies into the effects of stress and found that it had a significant impact on many gastro-intestinal disorders and also on other diseases such as asthma, diabetes, heart problems, some forms of rheumatoid arthritis, many cancers and even our propensity to get colds.[5] We saw in Chapter 2 that diet plays an important role in our health – stress has now been found to be an important factor too.

Another study demonstrated the correlation between stress and the tendency to get infections. Over a period of 12 months, 16 families kept diaries of stressful events. They also had throat cultures taken every three weeks or when they had acute infections. It was found that those individuals who were in acutely stressful situations were four times more likely to have a cold after the stress than beforehand. Where families were under more chronic stress, there was a higher incidence of infections than those with no stress.[6]

Another cause of stress is bereavement and the sadness and grief caused by it. This has also been found to influence our immune system.

Sadness and Grief

In 1975, 26 bereaved spouses were brave enough to take part in a study into the effect of stress on the immune system. They were tested two weeks after their bereavement and again six weeks later. A 'control' group made up of 26 people who had not been bereaved within the previous two years was also tested. The study showed clearly that the immune systems of those who were recently bereaved were severely suppressed whilst those of the control group remained normal.

The 26 bereaved spouses were more prone to illness during this extremely stressful period.[7] The Chinese believe that Grief and Sadness affect the lungs and the heart, as Pauline found:

> When my mum died I was low and lost a lot of weight. It knocked the
> stuffing out of me. I went down with a severe bout of pneumonia soon
> after and I'm sure the two were connected.

Infections are not the only problems to follow bereavement. The resulting suppressed immune system can cause cancer, arthritis, intestinal problems and many other conditions. Fortunately, counseling is now widely available for people who have undergone a bereavement or other Shock. The feelings could otherwise stay inside the person and cause illness later on in life.

In contrast, good feelings can delay the onset of illnesses. Charles says:

> I had good buddies and felt close to people during the time I was at college.
> I could turn up for the weekend course with a touch of flu and have no
> symptoms until I'd come back from it two days later. Many of the other
> people in my class had similar experiences.

Although good feelings can be beneficial to our health, Joy can also be a cause of disease.

Joy

We have seen the effects of laughter and positive emotions on our health so might wonder how Joy can have any negative effects. The Chinese understand that any extreme emotion can cause illness. Balance is the key word here. If we experience sudden and overwhelming feelings of Joy we can be left wide open. We may temporarily feel wonderful but our resistance to disease is lowered. If that dream of winning the lottery came true it might not be so good for our health!

An extreme form of Joy occurs when people become overexcited and manic. In this situation people may remain excessively Joyful and overactive for long periods of time. In time they can burn themselves out. Joy can also mean feeling 'up' but combined with feeling agitated and unsettled. The other side of this 'Joy' can be a sad and empty feeling. Many people laugh and show Joy to the world when inside they are deeply unhappy.

Our Attitude to our Emotions

Each individual has a different attitude to the traumatic life events they have gone through. Some people feel that they can never get over the upsets of the past. Others feel that they can learn from their problems and become better people for it. A counselor I know often works with people who are in severe distress. She commented to me:

> Some people have had a most appalling time in their lives and somehow
> manage to use it and learn from it. Others have had an awful time but seem
> to go round and round digging a deeper and deeper hole for themselves and
> not being able to get out.

So what are the differences that enable one person to be able to deal with their emotional difficulties and another not to? The answer to this is complex. The depth and intensity of the trauma, the timing of the difficulties in our lives, the length of time they continue are all relevant. How we deal with our problems is also important.

Common Stresses Through Stages of our Lives

Childhood 0–5

Lack of food; lack of warm environment; lack of emotional warmth and stimulation; lack of ability to get emotional needs met; lack of or too many physical boundaries; sibling rivalries; separating from parents as grow older.

Childhood 5–12

Starting school; making friends; learning difficulties; sibling rivalries; bullying; moving home; parents divorcing; keeping up with schoolwork; too much television.

Teenage years 13–19

Starting relationships with same or opposite sex; making friends; concern about appearance; fear of failing exams; difficulties choosing a career; becoming independent from parents; experimenting with drugs and/or alcohol; finding work; leaving home.

Adulthood 20–40

Finding a partner; building a home; starting a family; finding and settling in a career; financial worries and debts; competitive work situation; difficult boss; difficulties with colleagues; relationship problems; divorce.

Late Adulthood 40–60

Redundancies; lack of promotion; keeping up with changes in technology at work; caring for aging parents; family illness; death of relatives and friends; advancing age; poorer health; possible divorce.

Retirement 60+

Lack of feeling valued; deaths of loved ones; failing health; advancing age; failing eyesight, hearing, memory etc., loss of income; loss of ability to care for self; difficulty maintaining independence.

The Spectrum of our Emotional Traumas

The impact of emotions on our lives can vary according to the timing of the events. Events which took place in our childhood are likely to affect us more deeply than later traumas.

It is significant to note that children between the ages of five and nine who are experiencing the threat of loss within their family have been found to have an increased risk of diabetes and other serious illnesses.[8]

Traumas which take place later in life can also have a huge impact but don't usually go quite as deep as childhood events. The death of a loved one or the break-up of a relationship, for example, are shattering ordeals. These events are difficult to deal with but will usually heal over time if the person allows them to and gets the support they need.

Some emotions are more short-term than others. Feeling angry with our spouse for being late to a meal is one thing. Long-term, bottled-up Anger after continued mental or physical abuse is very different. It is easier to deal with emotional traumas in the present, then we will not have as many stuck emotions in the future. If we clear the Anger out of our system then we don't bottle-up more potential ill-health in the future.

In Part 2 of this chapter we will be looking at useful ways of managing our emotions.

Part Two
Dealing With Our Emotions

The famous Chinese medical textbook *The Yellow Emperor's Classic of Internal Medicine* says:[9]

Anger makes energy rise, Joy dissipates energy, Sadness dissolves energy,
Fear makes energy descend ... Shock scatters energy ... Worry knots energy.

When we respond negatively to a situation, our energy can become blocked or travel in the wrong direction. Once we express how we feel and get over the incident our energy is restored to its normal flow. Finding ways to keep our Qi flowing smoothly throughout our system will allow us to be physically, mentally and spiritually balanced. We can then deal with any crisis or emotional upheaval more easily.

So what are the best ways to deal with our emotions? The remainder of this chapter has many suggestions which form into three main groupings:

1 Ways to stay optimistic and positive. This will enable us to cope and lighten the load of stress. We can use these suggestions in our daily life.
2 Ways of dealing with emotions which are building up inside us. These suggestions are useful when a crisis occurs.
3 Other aspects of our lifestyle and how they can help us to remain balanced and deal with our emotions more positively.

I have taken these suggestions from many sources. Some are modern ways of dealing with emotions, others are older and derived directly from the Chinese culture. All are written in the 'spirit' of Chinese medicine and the understanding that resolving emotional problems can prevent disease.

The Power of Taking Pleasure from the World

How to stay contented

In the Ming dynasty, which started in 1368, a scholar named Wang Xunan suggested that we could stay contented by 'taking pleasure from the world'. He said that this in turn would enable us to have a long and happy life.[10] We can take pleasure in many simple things such as reading a book, walking in the countryside, feeling a warm breeze, admiring beautiful paintings, taking pleasure in music or looking at beautiful flowers. These are all opportunities to appreciate life.

One way to help us to take pleasure in life, on a daily basis, is to keep a daily journal. In this journal we can write down three things each day in answer to the following questions.

Keeping a journal

In the morning on waking we can ask ourselves:

- What do I appreciate in my life at present?
- What am I enjoying about my life at present?

In the evening we can then ask ourselves:

- What have I learned from today?
- What have I given out today?

If we do this regularly we will soon start to see life from a new perspective. Joan, who writes a journal, told me:

> I write a journal every day. It keeps me calm when disasters seem to be about to strike. Sometimes I write about exceptional things and at other times more mundane ones. It may be that I'm grateful for a happy relationship or just that I've made a decent supper. On Sunday I helped a friend and I appreciated that she wanted my help. Sometimes I'm just grateful for clarity of mind.

The Power of Keeping in Good Humor

Keeping in good humor is another powerful way of staying healthy. Norman Cousins was one of the first to write about the power of good humor. In his book *Anatomy of an Illness,* he describes how he cured himself of a life-threatening disease. Whilst in hospital his health deteriorated rapidly.

Eventually, he discharged himself, rented a hotel room and laughed at the Marx brothers' and other comedies all day. The laughter restored his health. He believes that he would not have recovered had he stayed in hospital.[11]

The 'Six always' to create a positive mind

The Chinese have known about the power of a positive state of mind for thousands of years. During the Ming dynasty, Shi Tianji, a Chinese scholar, wrote about the 'Six always' for maintaining a calm and cheerful state of mind.[12] He proposed:

1 That we always remain peaceful in mind – the less desires or hopes for personal gain we have, the more peaceful we will become.
2 That we always be kind-hearted – this will help us to gain pleasure from helping other people. If we always think about how others will benefit from what we do then we will have a tranquil mind and a clear conscience.
3 That we always uphold justice – if we hold fast to our integrity in all matters we will be clear about what is right or wrong for us.
4 That we always be cheerful – have a good laugh whenever possible.
5 That we always be pleasant – if we are amiable when dealing with others we will bring happiness to them and ourselves.
6 That we always be contented – although we can't avoid adversity we can strive to remain cheerful when there are troubles.

Shi Tianji recommended that we develop an attitude of looking on the 'bright side of life'. This can certainly help us through many difficulties. To carry out all of these suggestions perfectly would be impossible. Nevertheless, they are a good example of what we can strive towards in order to live happily.

Humor when we have difficulties

If we endeavor to have a laugh whenever possible it will take us a long way towards achieving contentment. The golden rule is to only ever laugh at our own expense and never at another's. Keeping a good sense of humor can support us through a crisis, as Julian found out.

My wife and I had been away on holiday and came back to find our house had been robbed. Much of our recently bought computer equipment had been taken. As we miserably looked around the house two things happened. Firstly, we discovered that some of the equipment had been left behind. We felt ecstatic! Secondly we looked at each other standing in shorts and tee-shirts in the middle of winter and started to laugh. It put it all in perspective. OK it wasn't great – but we'd had a good holiday and we'd cope.

We have talked about how taking pleasure from the world and staying in good humor can keep us positive and help us to remain in better health. Another way to keep optimistic is to develop a positive image of ourselves.

The Power of Developing a Positive Attitude

Interestingly, the Chinese word for a crisis is made up of two characters. One means 'danger' and the other means 'opportunity'. Embedded within the Chinese language and culture is the belief that opportunity arises out of our difficulties. By believing this, we can start to feel positive about our ability to deal with any situation.

Learning from our difficulties

A simple procedure we can use to develop this viewpoint is to learn to 're-frame' whatever situations come our way. This will in turn develop our good feelings about ourselves. Mistakes literally become opportunities to learn and difficulties seen as opportunities for change. We then find out that there is 'no failure only feedback'.[13] We feel better about ourselves as we begin to learn from our mistakes. Try repeating this simple sentence to yourself every time you are in difficulty:

- What can I learn from this?

If we make 'an error of judgment' it turns into an opportunity for greater understanding. If we do something 'wrong', the wrong doing will become something we can change next time around. The more we ask ourselves 'What can I learn from this?' the more we see ourselves in a positive light. Instead of being a person who does things badly, makes mistakes and is generally 'not good enough', we become a person who feels good about who we are as we are learning from our circumstances.

A positive self image

Evidence from research suggests that the better we feel about ourselves, the more mentally healthy we become. In fact, some studies show that healthy people 'have an enviable capacity to distort reality in a direction that enhances self-esteem, maintain beliefs in their personal efficacy and promote an optimistic view of the future'.[14]

'Mentally healthy' people have been found to have the ability to care about themselves and others, the ability to be happy and contented and the ability to engage in productive and creative work. Shelley Taylor has written a paper on 'Illusion and Well-being' and says that mentally well-adjusted people will often think of themselves as better than others but also see their closest friends and intimates more positively too. The more we can accept our positive side and see ourselves in a favorable way, the more we will maintain good health.

So far, we have looked at ways of remaining positive in order to keep our emotions in harmony. Sometimes we are affected by circumstances that cause us to become stuck in our feelings. The next four suggestions are ones we can use in these circumstances.

Dealing with 'Stuck' Emotions

If we fully experience our emotions when they arise we can usually clear them from our system. Often the negative emotions we encounter started when we were young. We may have been told 'Don't cry', 'Put on a brave face' or 'Don't get angry' or we may have merely copied our parents as they groped for ways of dealing with their own emotions. We internalized these constraints and examples and later no longer allowed ourselves to show our true feelings.

Learning from past events helps us to resolve any emotional blocks resulting from them. If we do not learn from them, similar situations will then bring up the same feelings again and again. An emotional 'pattern' occurs. Often we may blame other people who have said or done things which bring up these emotions. The more we take responsibility for our lives, the more we realize that we are reacting because we have unhealed emotional wounds.

One important ingredient can help us to deal with the emotional reactions we have. This is to temporarily separate ourselves from what we are experiencing. Techniques for doing this are suggested below. This distance allows us to understand our feelings better. Often this enables us to learn from what we have experienced and to move on.

The Chinese oracle *I Ching* or *Book of Changes* is around 4,000 years old. It has some wise words to say:[15]

> Difficulties and obstructions throw a man back on himself. While the inferior man seeks to put the blame on other persons, bewailing his fate, the superior man seeks the error within himself and through this introspection the external obstacle becomes for him an occasion for inner enrichment and education.

Gaining Perspective on our Emotions

This next exercise is especially helpful if we are having difficulty dealing with other people. It will literally enable us to find a new perspective on our situation.

Seeing different points of view

1 Find a quiet space where you can relax.
2 Think about the situation you are having difficulty with and imagine you are going through it again. See what you saw when it was happening, hear what you heard and feel any emotions involved. Especially see the other person and notice their breathing, posture, facial expression, gestures and voice tone.
3 Now imagine you are looking at the situation from the point of view of a neutral observer. Play an imaginary film of what is happening. Notice from your objective position both what the other person is saying and doing and also how you are responding. Observe how both you and the other person trigger each other's reactions. Gently ask yourself, 'What is the truth of this situation?'
4 Now see things from the perspective of the other person. Imagine you are that person and can feel as they feel. Gently ask yourself how does this person experience me?
5 You have now considered all positions. Go back to your original feelings and notice if you feel differently about them. You may have found new ways of dealing with the situation.

The three perspectives

When we are in conflict it can be easy to look at things only from our own point of view. Our own viewpoint is called '1st Position'. In this position, most of us blame others for any problems. The view of a person we are with (and may be in conflict with) is 2nd Position. It is much harder to see things from another person's perspective until we have seen the whole situation. Seeing the circumstances from a distance is the 3rd Position. It is also sometimes known as the position of the 'wise observer' as it is often from this position that we can get in touch with the truth of a situation and find useful ways of dealing with it.[16]

Lynn often uses this method. She told me:

Whenever I get wound up about something I stop myself and look at it from a distance. Now things don't tick away inside me waiting to explode. It's helped me to let go of things that would have been more difficult to let go of. I only needed to do it once or twice before it was easy to do.

Another way of gaining perspective on what is going on in our lives is by getting support through talking to other people.

Talking and Writing Therapy

Talking therapy

Linda Chih Ling Koo, in her book *Nourishment of Life,* about life in Chinese society wrote that:[17]

The traditional family structure served to provide support for the individual. Personal secrets were frequently solely shared between siblings or cousins ... between husbands and wives and between grandparents and children. These conversational and intimate exchanges allowed family members to release emotional tensions, to have disputes settled by a third party family member and to reaffirm their self worth because of the emphatic feelings expressed by their confidante.

The benefits of talking

When we are feeling angry, sad, fearful or grief-stricken there is nothing better than being able to talk to another person in order to release our deeply held feelings. Afterwards, we often feel much better just for having talked. Janice said:

> If I'm feeling tired and don't seem to improve after taking rest there's always
> an unexpressed emotion that needs to be teased out! I often then tease it out
> by talking it through with friends. Generally it then easily blows through.

The most important part of 'talking therapy' is to find a listener who will hear us without giving advice. Once our problem is out in the open and we feel heard, we may understand it better and it may recede on its own.

This is Jill's experience:

> It's incredibly relieving and reassuring to know someone else knows about
> my difficulties. It reduces the scale of the problem and puts it in perspective.
> Once I've told someone about it and know I've been heard, it instantly feels
> more manageable and that I can cope with it.

People in China often won't talk to 'strangers' about their problems. In the West, where family ties are less strong, we may decide to go to a counselor or therapist. Alternatively, it may be enough to talk to a friend. Bear these points in mind when choosing someone to talk to:

- Make sure you trust the person you talk to. If you suspect that the person is going to give away your deepest secrets then you will be unable to open up to them.
- Only talk to someone you have rapport with and can understand you.
- The person must be able to listen to you without giving you a 'solution'.
- You may like advice sometimes. Make an agreement with the listener to only give advice or a solution if you specifically ask for it.

Writing therapy

Sometimes it's hard to talk about our problems, so why not write them out? Writing can help us to resolve feelings or thoughts which have become stuck in our consciousness – especially if we find it difficult to talk about them. Here is one useful way of writing about our feelings:

- Find a place to write where you'll be comfortable and won't be disturbed.
- Write about your situation or problem for about 10-15 minutes continuously – don't think about your writing style or grammar.
- Completely let go and say anything and everything you want.
- Explore the whole situation. Write about it objectively (what actually happened) as well as subjectively (your feelings from your point of view).
- Feel free to let out your deepest feelings – don't plan to show anyone else – it will effect your ability to say whatever you want – make *yourself* your audience.

After writing you may feel relieved and immediately better or you may feel a little depressed or sad for a while. Don't worry about any negative feelings – they'll pass within an hour or two and be replaced by a new perspective on your life.

You can keep what you have written in the form of a journal or diary. Alternatively you can throw the letter or writing away or even make a ritual of burning the paper to show you have cleansed the problem from your psyche.

The Power of Positive Goals

Buddhist monks who meditated in the Tien Tai mountains in the Shixuan province of China hundreds of years ago had a specific method of dealing with their negative emotions. When thoughts came into their heads while they were meditating they became conscious of these thoughts – then thought of something which was opposite. For example, if they were thinking negatively about someone they would find something about them which was positive or if they were thinking about something which was a problem for them they would try to imagine it solved in the future. By doing this they could once more find tranquility in their meditation.[18]

Like Tien Tai monks, we too can find ways to retrain our minds to think positively. One way of doing this is by constructing positive goals for ourselves.

Noticing our negative beliefs

If we listen to the recurring thoughts which go through our heads we will find some thoughts that come back repetitively. These can be thoughts such as, 'I'll never get what I want in life', 'Don't trust anybody – they'll only let you down' or 'I always fail at everything I do'. Negative thoughts tend to become self-fulfilling prophesies bringing with them emotional turmoil and possible ill-health.

Sometimes just one negative thought can be at the root of many negative experiences but we may be unconscious of the thought. For example we may think 'The good times will all go wrong'. As a result of this we may notice that every time we are enjoying ourselves or doing something successfully we may feel anxious and unsettled but don't know why. At other times we may be more conscious of our negative thoughts but find it difficult to stop them. If we notice that we have a recurring negative thought it can be useful to turn it into a positive outcome or goal.

Six steps to constructing a positive goal

Our world is a manifestation of our thoughts, if we think negatively we will have negative experiences in our lives, if we think positively our life will become more positive. Recognizing our negative thoughts is the first step to translating them into something more positive.

Sometimes we already have an idea of what we want, but wish to fine tune it. Setting the goal and repeating it to ourselves will enable us to imagine what it will be like when we have what we want.

These are the golden rules to help us to construct a positive goal.

1 *Keep it in the present.* Rather than saying 'I will be successful' it is better to say I *am* successful. If this sounds too strong we might soften the sentence by saying '*I allow myself* to be successful'. If the goal is not stated in the present it will continue to be in the future so will never happen.

2 *Keep it positive.* Do not construct a sentence which contains a negative word such as 'not' or 'no'. This is because the mind does not translate a negative word. The mind always thinks in pictures. For example, if we say 'I don't have insomnia', we can't picture it. On the other hand if we say 'I allow myself to have deep and nourishing sleep at night', we can picture ourselves deeply asleep at the end of the day.

3 *Keep it simple and achievable.* A goal which has too many parts becomes complicated and is less likely to manifest. For example, if we say 'I allow myself to have a good job, a house, a car and a good relationship' we are diluting the possibilities of achieving any of these things. If we stop to think about what's behind wanting these things and realize, for example, that we expect them to bring us contentment and peace, then it might be better to say 'I have the things which bring me contentment and peace'. It is then more likely that we will get what we want rather than what we *think* we want.

4 *Put yourself in the goal.* If you have a picture or sense of yourself achieving the goal it is best that you are seeing yourself having achieved it in order for it to manifest. For example, if you want to buy a new pair of trousers it is best to see yourself wearing the trousers. If you see the trousers but you are not wearing them they might be in a shop waiting for you but you might never find them!

5 *Focus on the end result not on the process of doing it.* Staying with the example above, if you imagine yourself shopping for trousers, you might wander around the shops all day but never find the pair of trousers you want. On the other hand if you see yourself wearing the new trousers you are more likely to get the outcome you desire.

Once you have constructed your outcome

6 *Consider what might happen if you did get the goal you desire.* Consider both the negative and the positive implications. If, for example, you state 'I allow myself to meet the person of my dreams' this might have many unwanted repercussions. The person of your dreams might live in another country, continually be unfaithful or have some bad habits you didn't predict. Think carefully about your goal and choose the wording of your goal with care!

June is convinced that she turned around how she dealt with her relationships through finding a positive goal. She told me:

'All my relationships fail' is what I constantly said to myself – especially when I met someone new. Inevitably, they did fail. I'd felt rejected a lot when I was young and I think this was why I had this thought. Over time I worked a lot on my self-image. One important affirmation I made was, 'I choose to have a loving and successful relationship'. I also wrote down all the qualities I wanted in a man. Within a few months I'd met someone new and we're still together a year later.

Once you have completed the six steps above, you will have constructed a positive outcome for yourself. You might remember it and repeat it to yourself or write it down. As you go over your goal it is useful to imagine what it will be like when you have it, as vividly as possible.

To further fine tune your goal you can take it one step further.

Releasing our negative thoughts

Sometimes we construct a positive goal but find our mind is still holding onto an underlying negative belief. The following is a way of releasing these negative thoughts:

1 Think of your positive goal and imagine what it's like to have it.
2 Check to see if any thought comes up which is contrary to you having what you want.
3 Welcome the thought.

4   Acknowledge that you have the right to have your goal and release the negative thought.

5   Repeat the procedure until the negative thoughts are cleared.

For example, you may have constructed a goal, 'I allow myself to have the perfect job for me'. You can then imagine what it will be like to be working in the perfect job and make it as real as possible. When you check to see if any thoughts are coming up which are contrary to this you might think, for example, 'I won't be able to – there are no jobs in this town'. You can then welcome this thought and say to yourself 'I acknowledge that I think I won't be able to find the perfect job as there are no jobs in town, but I'm choosing to let this thought go'. You can then consciously release it from your mind. You then picture once more how it will be when you have this goal and repeat the process until you feel confident that you can have this goal manifest in your life.

Discharging Blocked Feelings

So far we have discussed ways of acquiring insight into our emotions. Sometimes as we gain deeper awareness into our emotions they are resolved and we may start to cry or become more relaxed. At other times we may still have feelings inside and not know how to release them.

Stuck feelings

Blocked emotions often occur if it is difficult or inappropriate to express them when they arise. As a result we can remain feeling tense and frustrated or on the brink of tears. Stuck emotions cause the Qi to stop moving inside us. Activity allows the energy to move again – the emotional feelings then become less intense. All emotions need to be acknowledged including our Joy and good feelings but the emotions most often held back are Anger, Grief and Sadness.

In part of Taiwan an interesting method of expressing emotions was developed. Individuals would go to a secluded spot in the early hours of the morning and laugh, scream, shout, cry or talk to no one in particular. This would allow them to release their pent-up feelings so that the stuck Qi could begin to circulate again. After several minutes they felt more relaxed and calm and equilibrium was restored to their systems.[19]

If emotions are stuck inside us we can try this method used in Taiwan to release them and find a place where we can cry, shout, scream and generally release our emotions. Many of us don't realize we are bottling up our feelings, but we know that we are not moving forward in life. For others it can be difficult to readily let the feelings out. In this case, physical activity can also help us to clear stuck emotions.

Physical activity to move our emotions

Activity can be anything from going for a run or a vigorous walk, playing tennis or other racquet games, skipping or even jumping up and down or stamping the feet. Banging on drums can also be a useful way of releasing feelings. Other people release feelings by beating a cushion with their fists. I have heard that some work places in Japan even have a punch bag outside the washroom. The workers can hit it to release any frustration – then continue with their work in a more positive frame of mind! To induce unshed tears we can watch a weepy film or read a moving book. As we start to cry we can free up the stuck tears and Sadness.

Clearing emotions can be an important release, but they will recur unless we also deal with the underlying causes. We can be angry for many reasons. These can include not feeling appreciated, feeling frightened, not feeling respected or feeling unloved. Forgiveness, for example, can be an essential ingredient for resolving Anger – otherwise it may never be fully cleared. We sometimes need to use a combination of approaches in order to get to the source of our emotions. While it is beyond the scope of this book to describe all of the ways available, the techniques described can be extremely helpful.

Our emotional balance is also linked to our overall health.

Lifestyle and our Emotions

When we are ill our emotions easily become out of balance. We know that when a baby is sick it cries and becomes fretful or more irritable. In the same way we become easily upset or irritated when we are unwell. Caring for our overall lifestyle can enable us to keep healthy emotionally.

Our organ 'functions' and our emotions

Chinese medicine teaches that Anger, for instance, affects the functioning of the Liver. The opposite is also true. If we have a Liver imbalance we will have greater difficulty dealing with issues of Anger. For example, if we are unhappy we may drink too much alcohol, then the Liver can become imbalanced. The more our Liver becomes affected, the more easily we become angry. In turn the Anger makes our Liver yet more out of balance. A vicious circle is set in motion.

Imbalances in the other organs affect our emotions in a similar way. Weakened Kidney energy will make us more fearful and imbalanced Lung energy more vulnerable to feelings of Grief and loss. Deficient Stomach and Spleen energy may cause us to Worry and have obsessional thoughts and imbalanced Heart energy can create Sadness, anxiety or inappropriate Joy.[20]

The more we keep in good health, the better our emotional balance. The better our emotional balance, the better our health. A positive cycle of health will then develop.

Ann felt better emotionally when she changed her lifestyle:

> I used to be very anxious. I'd panic for no reason just walking down the street. If I thought of something scary, I'd jump inside. When I went to a practitioner of Chinese medicine he told me that it was to do with my Heart Blood which was so deficient that I couldn't feel settled inside. He gave me some treatment but also advised me to eat Blood nourishing food (*see page 25*) and to do some gentle Qigong exercises. It's made a big difference. I'm much better now and only occasionally get mildly anxious.

Qigong and our emotions

Practicing Qigong can sometimes help to clear our blocked emotions. The Chinese understood that when our Qi is imbalanced it effects us on all levels – physically, mentally, spiritually and emotionally. If our feelings are stuck inside us this will be reflected in our bodies. As we practice Qigong and physically release areas which are tense or blocked we may also clear bottled up emotions. In Chapter 4 we will discuss Qigong and find out more about an exercise for clearing stuck emotions and other negativity.

Chinese Medicine and our Emotions

Some of us may feel too unwell to deal with our emotional condition on our own. In this case we may choose to get the support of a counselor or therapist or find other professional help. An alternative choice may be to go to visit an acupuncturist, Chinese herbalist or another practitioner of Chinese medicine. Val who is 39 and has three children found it changed every area of her life:

> Before I had acupuncture I didn't feel close to my children – I always used to push them away. Since I've had treatment I feel a new love and closeness to them. My marriage is also stronger. Before I was always uppity with my husband. I used to have PMT too – now one week before my period I feel only a little stressed. Having treatment has changed my outlook 100 per cent.

Although Val now feels different, she also knows that she needs to look after her lifestyle to remain healthy.

> I just used to grab anything for my meals. Now I always stop and give myself a break rather than eating on the run. I think about what I'm going to have for lunch – and I take much more warm food instead of just grabbing a sandwich. I also drink a lot more water and I rarely have coffee. Things taste better and there's an amazing difference in my skin and hair. I also walk as much as I can. It's given me so much confidence I can walk into a room and not give a damn.

The healthier we become, the better we can deal with any new difficulties. If we are unhealthy, we are often at the mercy of the emotions we feel. When we are healthy, we can feel strong enough to find new ways of dealing with life events instead of reacting from our negative patterns.

In the following chapters we will be looking at more ways to achieve good health through lifestyle.

Summary

1   Laughter and optimism can have positive effects on our health.
2   Emotions tend to cause disease when they are extremely prolonged or intense, or if they are not expressed or acknowledged.
3   The Chinese call our emotions the Internal causes of disease. They are: Anger, Fear, Joy, Shock, Worry, Grief or Sadness. These seven emotions include all other emotions.
4   Being positive will enable us to cope with stress more easily. Three ways we can do this are:
    • Appreciating life's pleasures and writing a journal about them.
    • Finding humor in difficult situations.
    • Asking ourselves what we can learn from our situation.
5   We can learn to deal with any stuck emotions. Four of the many ways we can do this are:
    • Distancing ourselves from our emotions and seeing them in perspective.
    • Finding positive goals for ourselves.
    • Using 'talking therapy'.
    • Expressing our emotions or using activity to release them.
6   If we look after the other aspects of our lifestyle, the resulting good health will positively affect the way we feel. Acupuncture, herbs or other Chinese therapies can also help us to deal with emotions.

The Secret of How to Work, Rest and Exercise

When I was in China I was fascinated by the way people worked, rested and exercised. They know the secret of keeping a balance in their daily lives in order to stay healthy. In the early morning, for example, large numbers of people go to the parks to practice Tai Ji Quan or Qigong exercises. These exercises are designed to develop the mind as well as the body. Those not out in the parks are likely to be exercising inside their homes. Most people have their own favorite healthy routine and their practice prepares them for the day ahead.

Having exercised, most Chinese travel to work by bike. In the urban areas, thousands of Chinese people can be seen cycling to work during the bicycle 'rush hour' in the morning. Cycling gives them vigorous exercise and is a healthy way of getting to work.

Later, in the middle of the day, it's common to see people taking a short nap after they've eaten their lunch. Like those in Mediterranean countries, Chinese people know the benefits of a long break for lunch. Workers fall asleep in their carts, office workers put their heads down at their desks and the elderly doze on roadside seats. After lunch and a rest they are ready and fresh for work in the afternoon.

As well as having a siesta during the lunch-break, rest time is also taken after work. Chinese people say that about one-third of the time spent working should be spent relaxing. This could be anything from socializing with friends, playing with the children, having a gentle walk, reading or taking the midday nap described above. Some of this rest time is spent unwinding before going to bed.

Chinese people tend to go to bed fairly early. The hours before 12 o'clock give them their most nourishing sleep. At least eight hours of deep sleep is strengthening to their organs and replenishes their reserves of energy. They can then rise again the next morning ready to exercise.

Chinese medicine tells us that we need to alternate our work, relaxation and exercise and to get enough sleep. Finding a routine which balances these aspects of our life will enable us to become healthier and more contented with our lives.

In Part 1 of this chapter we will consider our working habits and the Chinese view of exercise. In Part 2 we will look at the Chinese attitude to sleeping and the importance of relaxation.

Part One
Work and Exercise

Work and rest must be balanced. The Chinese concept of balance comes from the famous Yin/Yang symbol shown below.

Figure 3: The Yin/Yang symbol.

Yin and Yang describe two qualities in our lives which are constantly interacting. Yang is active, warm and moving in nature whilst Yin is passive, cool and calm. Although these two energies are opposites they also depend on each other.

Many Westerners lead lifestyles which are out of balance. Some are far too Yang and overactive, others lead a lifestyle which is too Yin and underactive. When the movement and rest in our lifestyle is out of harmony we start to create ill-health and dissatisfaction within ourselves.

Balancing our Work, Rest and Exercise

It is best that we balance our work, relaxation, exercise and sleep within each 24-hour cycle. This means that we don't work for weeks at a time without a break nor do we overexercise until we are exhausted. Many people are far too mentally overactive and stressed at work – their lifestyle is often too Yang. Others have a lifestyle which is too static and Yin.

Yin and Yang and lifestyle

If our lifestyle is too Yang and overactive we may find ourselves doing things like:

- working through our lunch-break without stopping
- overriding feelings of tiredness and continuing working
- feeling obliged to work late
- going back to work before we have fully recovered from illness
- continually juggling so many things that we never stop.

If we are in the habit of overworking it can even be difficult for us to stop and take notice because we are far too busy. If, on the other hand, our lifestyle is too Yin and static we may find ourselves:

- spending a large proportion of the day sitting
- feeling tired even though we've been inactive
- driving to work when it would be easy to cycle or walk

- exercising less than once a week
- often feeling sluggish and a bit depressed.

Some people have a lifestyle which is too Yin or too Yang. Others have a mixture of underactivity and overactivity together. Some people, for instance, may drive to work when they could walk, in order to have more time to work harder. Others may spend time feeling exhausted and inactive then override this with frenetic activity and staying up too late in order to catch up. Any extreme is unhealthy and is better if it is tempered by a more balanced routine. Let's take a closer look at overactivity and underactivity.

Overwork

As success becomes the priority, health becomes less important and many people overwork in ways they never did before. As well as paying for the mortgage and other expenses, 'work' for some people is a source of status and self-esteem. The result is not making time to look after their health. Others fear losing their jobs or missing a well-deserved promotion if they are off sick.

Sue used to overwork. She told me:

> I think in all commercial organizations there is always a lot of change going on. The change happens fast and often. Where I was working everyone ended up chasing their own tails. It's hard not to get caught up in it. There was always the expectation to stay after 5pm for meetings and to eat lunch on the run. I think it's what goes on in many companies. There was also a juggling act of who's looking after the kids. In those 8–10 years I can't remember sleeping much as I used to feel guilty about stopping and resting – it was whiz whiz.

Like Sue, staying late at work and eating meals on the run has become part of the work ethos for many of us. If we are living unhealthily and don't find time to stop, then sometimes illness stops things for us.

Working when we are ill or convalescing

Becoming ill always carries a message with it. Often if we are overworking the message is that our body wants us to stop. It is now increasingly common for people to feel guilty if they take time off work to convalesce. The result is that many people go back to work before they have fully regained their health.

For Sue (who overworked) this was the result:

> When I first had a lump in my spine I went back to work before I'd even
> been signed off – I was so keen and thought myself indispensable! I think I
> depleted my energy even more in a negative way. My body did compensate
> and I could keep going but I was 'running on empty'. When I later got breast
> cancer I knew better – I took March to October off work.

Another common situation is people continuing to work hard when they still have the remains of an infection or virus in their system. Often the body becomes so weak that they can't throw it off. Later on, the person's whole system may give up and they find themselves unable to work at all. This can be the beginning of post-viral conditions like ME, which are very hard to cure.

This is what happened to Fiona:

> From 1985–93 I had periods of overworking. I was working in education – it
> was a demanding job and stressful. I got glandular fever and I didn't realize
> the importance of rest. I couldn't stay home from work because if I was away
> no one else would do it. No one encouraged me to take care of myself, it was
> more, 'Go back there and do it'. I was also encouraged to exercise when I was
> still ill rather than resting. The final straw was having a hysterectomy and not
> resting for long enough afterwards. I never recovered and got ME.

When we are ill we become tired easily because our body tells us it needs to rest in order to recover. Many of us have lost touch with these messages and no longer realize the importance of convalescing. Had Fiona known to rest when she was initially ill with glandular fever, she thinks she would be healthy today.

Convalescence used to be a normal stage of recovery from illness. At one time people also understood that they shouldn't exercise vigorously when ill. We now ignore our body messages at our peril. Post-viral syndromes are on the increase in Western society and will continue to be so until we go back to the convalescing habits of our predecessors. Taking time to rest will also prevent other serious conditions brought on by stressful lifestyles like Sue's.

Modifying an overactive lifestyle

If your lifestyle is overactive, here are some areas you might check:

- Are you getting enough rest time and breaks at work?
- Are you following a two-thirds work to one-third rest ratio?
- Are you planning rest time into your day?
- Do you have at least a small amount of time each day just for nourishing yourself?
- If you are ill do you take time to fully convalesce?

If the answer to most of these questions is 'no' then it's time to stop and take a serious look at our style of working. Continuing to overwork can lead to serious consequences on our health.

Finding fulfillment in our work

We can also ask ourselves if our work is enjoyable and worthwhile. If we have work which we enjoy and find fulfilling then it will have positive effects on our health. A small amount of stress can be stimulating but extreme stress will ultimately make us less productive. Unfulfilling or very boring work may also have negative consequences on our health.

Even if we don't like our work we can bring as many nourishing activities as possible into our day to lift ourselves. We may get ideas from this chapter or from Chapter 3 on emotions. The healthier we are and the better we feel in ourselves, the more we can enjoy what we do and feel less stressed by it. Looking after our lifestyle sometimes enables us to find more fulfillment from our job. For some, changing jobs may turn out to be the best decision. Feeling healthier may enable us to make the right choice.

One way of dealing with stress and generating good feelings inside is this exercise:

The Inner Smile

This is a well-known Chinese exercise and only takes a few minutes to do. It relaxes and rejuvenates the internal organs and helps us through any tense situation. We can do this exercise at any time – sitting in the office, in a stressful meeting or when studying for exams. It will make any difficulties easier to cope with.

1 Sit with your back straight.
2 Imagine seeing something that will make you smile. Allow yourself to smile internally – it doesn't have to be visible – only felt by you.
3 Allow the smile to shine out of your eyes.
4 Now let the smile travel downwards into all of your internal organs. Notice the feeling of relaxation generated by the internal smile.
5 Allow the smile to travel down to your Tan Tien which is just below the naval.
6 Carry on with what you are doing, keeping the feeling generated by the internal smile. Others will also respond to the good feelings activated by this internal smile.

Smiling internally is good preparation before starting Qigong exercises (*see page 91*).

Underactivity

While overwork is on the increase, exercise is on the decrease. Startling research shows that even children are less active than they once were. Research was carried out at Exeter University in 1994.[1]

Children and exercise

A study was made of 250 children over a period of one week. It found that 90 per cent of children between the ages of 10 and 16 were failing to do even the minimum weekly exercise recommended by health experts. One in five 10-year-old boys and nearly one in three girls did not even manage one brisk 10-minute walk in a week. By the time children had reached secondary school level they were even less active! The exercise habit starts young. 'In-active children turn into inactive adults,' says researcher Neil Armstrong. 'If we don't do something about improving levels of activity we are going to have problems in the future with obesity and heart disease.'

Physical work has now largely been replaced by desk jobs. Many people sit behind computers every day. Ann was typical of someone who was too inactive:

> I work in an office doing accounts. I used to drive to and from work and then often sit at a computer for most of the day. When I went home I was too tired to do anything and would just sit and watch television. After about two years I noticed that I'd put on weight and that my breathing was becoming shallow. I was also slightly depressed and suffered from insomnia on and off. My lifestyle had become too static.

Many of us are like Ann and are in sedentary jobs for a large part of the day. If we are relatively inactive in our daily routine we have to create time to exercise. People used to exercise while doing their daily work or traveling to or from work. For many of us now these habits have changed.

Exercising while we work

Laboring and farming jobs once involved muscle work. Much of this work has now been replaced by machinery. Daily housework was also a fairly active occupation. None of us would wish to go back to the days before the time of labor-saving devices such as vacuum cleaners and automatic wash-ing machines. If we did go back to that way of life, however, we would certainly be more active. Cycling or walking to work was also the norm at one time. Now we drive even short distances.

Bringing exercise into our life

Here are some different ways people bring physical exercise into their lives. Gill who is 49 walks her dog:

> I take my dog for a walk in the park for 40 minutes a day. Walking doesn't sound exciting but my tension levels abate. There's a certain briskness in my step and I walk up a hill for extra exercise.

Judy who is 37 said:

> For exercise I go horse riding. That is the one thing I absolutely always do twice a week regardless of how busy I am. I've done it for the past six years. I think it's really good for relaxing me and switching off my mind.

Margi who is in her 40s says:

> I cycle and walk. I have no car and it's been amazing for me. I'm fitter now than I've been for years. For a period of my life I was really tired. Before I'd look at a hill and think 'Oh no!' I would never exercise as I thought it was too much effort. Once I started I could do it easily.

If we are underactive, here are some other ways which we can bring exercise into our daily lives:

1 jogging to the shops
2 walking upstairs rather than taking a lift
3 parking some distance from the office and walking
4 cycling to work
5 going out dancing
6 gardening.

Some people prefer to take exercise in their homes and a carefully chosen exercise video may help them to structure a routine.

The benefits of exercise

Studies have found that regular exercise helps to improve our energy and significantly lower levels of anger, depression and tension.[2] Research also indicates that regular exercise throughout life can help to prevent osteoporosis.[3]

Exercise has also been proved to decrease the risk of heart disease. In 1980 a questionnaire evaluated the daily physical activity of 17,944 middle-aged British civil servants. Eight years later a follow up was given. It was found that the incidence of heart disease was 50 per cent less in those who had a more active lifestyle.[4]

Internal and External Exercise

The Chinese distinguish between two types of exercise – External and Internal.

External exercise

External exercise is any exercise which focuses primarily on strengthening the body. Exercises carried out in the West are often of this type. They include running, cycling, swimming or playing other sports. In China, 'harder' style martial arts like Kung-Fu also come into this category. External exercises emphasize strengthening the physical body and can be quite vigorous. Although they do affect our general well-being, there is no emphasis on the mental and spiritual aspects of a person.

Internal exercise

Internal exercises are different. They focus on movements which activate the inside of our body and our organs rather than purely external movement. Internal exercises tend to be gentler than External ones. Qigong and Tai Ji Quan (*see page 91*) come under this heading. Other Internal exercises are yoga and 'soft' martial arts like aikido. The result of doing these Internal exercises is that we develop internal strength and become calmer and healthier from within.

Chinese medicine teaches that Internal and External exercises are beneficial to our health and understands the need for both.

How much exercise do I need?

There is no standard amount of activity and rest. How much we need depends on our age, build and constitution and how much activity we take during the rest of the day. If our work is not balanced between mental and physical activity we can redress this imbalance by the way we exercise. For most adults, 20 to 30 minutes of External physical activity, three times a week, is a good minimum. Internal exercises are best practiced daily – we'll discuss this in more detail on pages 91–101.

Finding a routine

It is best to have a routine for any exercise that we do. If we get into a regular habit we will then continue to practice. Most people begin exercising with great enthusiasm – maintaining the habit when the initial 'high' has gone is more of a challenge. Remember what we said in Chapter 1. It takes a month to change a habit – so stick with it. Once we have exercised regularly for a month it will easily become a part of our everyday routine.

Here's what Ann, who had been too inactive, did:

> As I always drove into work, the first change I made was to cycle instead.
> It took me 15 minutes to cycle into work by a river rather than a 10-minute
> drive caught in traffic. Once I had started it was easy to continue. As I was
> sitting for most of the day I also decided to get up more frequently and walk
> around. This was harder to remember to do so I did some simple stretching in
> these breaks. In the evening I did a 15-minute Qigong exercise. This helped
> me to sleep. Within a few weeks my breathing was feeling easier and I was
> much happier in myself. I've kept up the routine and, combined with a
> healthy diet, I've now lost quite a bit of weight too.

Ann made changes she knew she could keep up. We don't usually need to make big adjustments. Research shows that even a little exercise can go a long way. A report from the United States Surgeon General says that a brisk walk for 30 minutes, waxing and washing a car for 45–60 minutes or pushing a pram for one and a half miles in 30 minutes is enough to reduce depression and anxiety and cut the risk of illness. A scheme to encourage Americans to exercise, called Exercise Lite, suggests 20 minutes of exercise three days a week as a minimum.[5]

Overexercising

Too much exercise can be as harmful to our health as too little. Like over-working, exercising until we drop or doing overly vigorous exercise is more likely to deplete our energy than to increase our health.

It is always best to function at less than our full capacity. The Chinese emphasize balance and suggest moderation with respect to everything we do. Over straining when we exercise can lead to injury, tension or over taxing our system. The net result of this is not better health – in fact we are more likely to feel worse and finally stop the activity altogether.

The '70 per cent' rule

In his Qigong book, *Opening the Energy Gates of your Body*, Bruce K Frantzis describes this as the '70 per cent rule' and says:

> First estimate what 100% of your physical capacity is in terms of range of movement or time of practice; that is, how far your body can actually endure before it collapses. Once you determine this, you then only move or practice to 70% of your capacity. This percentage is not rigid, and the appropriate amount could be anywhere from 60% to 80%, depending on your constitution.[6]

Bruce Frantzis then goes on to suggest that we regularly remind ourselves of the 70 per cent rule. It is important never to push the body into activity that it doesn't wish to do or to go beyond our limits. If we feel exhausted by our exercise or don't enjoy doing it, then it is not right for us.

Paul used to exercise too much:

> I used to go running and at one time I ran myself into the ground and overtrained. I remember having sleepless nights as my body couldn't slow

down. I was just focusing myself on training even though I hadn't recovered from the night before. I've learnt in the last few years that exercise and rest equals strength. I now coach my son doing competitive mountain biking. Since he cut down from five days a week to three, he's working better and progressing more.

Activity, Rest, Age and Constitution

At the beginning of our lives we are normally very Yang. Yang activity is very outgoing and we move from being energetic children to active adults. Later in life we naturally become more Yin and may wish to slow down. It is very common in the West for people to ignore this move from Yang to Yin energy and not to listen to their body's messages. As a result, many people, especially women when they come into menopause, are overworking when they should be slowing down.

Overactivity uses up our calming and cooling Yin energy and results in symptoms like hot flushes and feelings of agitation. A certain amount of vigorous exercise is useful earlier in our life, especially if we have a strong constitution (*see Chapter 6*). If we are older or frailer we might prefer to do more gentle, Internal exercises.

Our body type will also indicate what is the right kind of exercise for us. People with large, strong bodies often wish to do more External exercise than those who have smaller, frailer bodies. Those with smaller body types still need activity but can do less and often prefer the more Internal type.

Qigong exercises are ones that can be practiced by all people of every age and body type.

Qigong Exercises and their Benefits

Qigong and Tai Ji Quan are Internal exercises. They are rapidly becoming popular in the West. 'Qi' means energy and 'gong' means practice. These exercises activate our Qi. Qigong has a significant effect on improving our health and maintaining our well-being. It also helps us to develop mentally and spiritually and will clear stress, remove tension and help us to relax. In general, the exercises are performed by moving in a slow and relaxed way, while at the same time maintaining a good posture. Some movements are performed while standing still, others are done while gently moving.

Qigong and our health

There are many different styles of Qigong and teachers will all have their own unique method. If practiced well, all styles will have an overall positive effect on our health and well-being. As far back as 200 BC Chinese doctors realized that gentle exercise can stimulate the flow of our Qi. When our Qi runs smoothly throughout our bodies we remain healthy. If our Qi is blocked or weakened this can lead to ill-health. Some exercises improve our health in a general way by creating a better balance of Qi throughout our system. This can also lead to greater feelings of contentment and well-being. Others are specifically designed to improve the functioning of different organs in the body such as the Kidney, Liver, Lung or Heart. Others are aimed directly at other functions such as helping the digestive system, improving the circulation or clearing the head.

Joy says:

> When I was a teacher and a mother I realized that I had no time of my own so I got up half an hour earlier to be by myself. At this time I exercise regularly doing Qigong exercises. I feel that it's part and parcel of toning me and it also starts up my day and gives me a focus. If I don't do it I'm all helter-skelter.

James told me:

> My body is in much better shape since I've done Qigong. It's looser and I'm therefore more upright. My chest is softer and easier and my shoulder, which has been a problem for 30 years, is enormously better. I'm over 60 and I haven't stiffened up in the way I might have – it makes everything a little smoother and easier. I also feel more vitality from doing it and I have more comfort in my body.

A Qigong Stretch

This exercise is a complete stretch. It strengthens all of the internal organs and stretches the spine to help back problems. Practicing it daily will strengthen breathing and help to create a smooth flow of Qi throughout the body.

1 Stand relaxed with the feet shoulder width apart, knees slightly bent and feet facing forwards. Place the hands about one and a half inches below the navel, palms facing downwards and with the fingers pointing towards each other.
2 Breathe in, imagining that you are taking vital, pure Qi into your body. At the same time bring the hands outwards and upwards in front of the body so that the palms are held high above the head facing upwards. Look up and at the same time stretch the palms of the hands upwards, keeping the back straight.
3 Breathe out and at the same time lower the hands out to the sides while bending the knees slightly. Imagine that you are clearing any stale or impure Qi through the fingers.
4 Bring the hands back to the starting position.
5 Repeat this exercise at least 10 times every day. The benefits will be felt from it only if it is performed on a regular basis.

Figures 4a, 4b, 4c: A Qigong stretch.

Three Important Principles for Qigong Practice

All Qigong techniques emphasize a focused mind, good posture and relaxation. By affecting our Qi they balance us physically, mentally and spiritually, which in turn leads to better health. We'll look at each principle in turn.

A focused mind

There is a saying that 'where the mind goes our energy follows' and this is certainly true when it comes to Qigong practice. When we practice Qigong our mind needs to be fully involved in it and at the same time remain relaxed and calm. If the mind is directed inwards we may scan our bodies from top to bottom and notice areas of tension, contraction or numbness. By focusing on these areas we can begin to release our internal blockages and awaken the flow of Qi in our bodies. We can also imagine holding a large ball between the hands. The ball may be kept still or be slowly moved upwards, downwards, from side to side or rotated backwards or forwards. This can also help to direct the energy. Alternatively, an exercise may be carried out while putting the attention on the Tan Tien (a place approximately three finger widths below the navel). More is written about the Tan Tien in Chapter 7.

Good posture

When standing or sitting it is important that our posture is upright and the spine remains straight. This is aided by aligning the body so that our weight can travel downwards from the middle of the spine through the hips and into the arches of our feet. The base of the spine should point downwards towards the feet. The upper body should have a slight upward lift through the middle and upper spine and into the neck and head. The head should feel as if it is floating slightly above the neck allowing the head to be upright. The chest should be slightly hollowed but not collapsed. The better our posture, the more fluidly our Qi can flow through our system. This will in turn enhance our health and well-being on every level.[7] For more on standing posture see Chapter 7, page 148.

Relaxation

All Qi exercises are carried out by slowing down inside, softening and becoming relaxed. This relaxation allows the energy to smoothly circulate through the body which in turn enhances our vitality. The relaxation of Qigong and other Internal exercises is very alive and dynamic because our mind is focused as we relax.

Combining a focused mind, good posture and relaxation when we exercise enhances the experience we have. This can result in improvements to our health and often means we finish our practice with an inner sense of well-being.

Exercising in the 'Spirit' of Qigong

All Qigong is practiced by emphasizing the three important principles above. Any exercise can be done in the 'spirit' of Qigong using these principles. This is in direct contrast to the way exercise is often practiced, which is, with tension and speed rather than relaxation and softness, by paying attention only to the body rather than to our body *and* how it feels internally and with a bad posture rather than with a posture that will enhance our energy flow. Exercising in the spirit of Qigong will enhance the quality of the exercises we do and therefore create more positive benefits from them.

A Cleansing Qigong Exercise

This exercise is for cleansing us of negative energy. This includes any illness or negative emotions which we want to clear from our system.

1 Stand with the feet shoulder width apart and arms by the sides.
2 Slowly allow the arms to rise up above the head so that the hands are back to back.
3 Turn the palms to face each other. Stretch the arms up to the sky. Imagine the space between the arms is like a tumbler filling up with water and that the higher the arms stretch up to the heavens the more water fills the tumbler ready to cleanse you.
4 When the 'tumbler' is full, bend the wrists inwards so that the palms are facing down.
5 Bring the hands slowly downwards sensing the water cleansing through the body and allowing first the head, then the body, to emerge cleansed.
6 When the water gets below the ribs, point the hands down feeling the water cleansing through the legs and feet and into the ground.
7 Shake the hands to cleanse any remaining negativity. Repeat this exercise at least 5–10 times.

Figures 5a, 5b, 5c, 5d, 5e, 5f: A cleansing Qigong exercise.

The more this exercise is done, the less time it will take to cleanse blocks to our Qi.[8]

Learning Qigong

For those who are seriously interested in practicing Qigong, the best way to start is by finding a good teacher. A teacher will adjust our posture and guide us to practice the exercises correctly and safely. A teacher will also show us some exercises which we can then practice at home in our own time. The best way of finding a teacher is by word of mouth – make sure that the teacher you go to is highly recommended by existing students.

How Much Qigong should I do?

Many people like to do half an hour of Qigong practice daily – some practice more. It is better to practice a small amount regularly than a larger amount at irregular times. Fifteen minutes practiced every day is better than a three-hour session at irregular intervals.

Seven Tips for Creating an Exercise Routine

Although there is no one form of exercise which is right for everyone, there are certain points we can look at in order to make changes towards a healthier routine.

1 Decide on how you would like to exercise and when you will do it – write it down. Make it a part of your routine.
2 Plan exercise into your day. If you have a list of things to do, put it on the list.
3 If necessary make compromises – sometimes you may need to give up an activity to make way for a healthier change. For example you may decide to leave work earlier to go to the gym or to do gentle Qigong exercises before bed instead of watching television.
4 Make small changes slowly and try to incorporate them into the lifestyle you have now.
5 Do exercises which you find enjoyable. If you don't enjoy your exercises they won't benefit you – find other exercises which you like.
6 Don't over strain or over exercise – this leads to tension and depletes rather than enhances our energy.
7 Remember it takes a month to fully integrate changes into our lives.

Here is a Qigong exercise which you may wish to practice in the morning. It can of course be performed at any time, but is especially useful to prepare you for the day ahead.

A Morning Qigong Exercise – Patting the Body

This is a simple exercise which can have profound effects. It is good for strengthening the tendons, bones and muscles, improving the circulation and enhancing the functioning of the internal organs. After patting the body we will feel wide awake, ready for action, clear headed and our spirits will be lifted. Patting is said to be more effective than massage performed by other people.

The whole body is lightly patted with either the palms or fists, in eight main areas. Before starting the exercise stand with the feet shoulder width apart and relax the whole body. Make sure that the knees are slightly bent and the feet are facing forwards. Breathe naturally as you do the exercise.

Pat the head

Pat both sides of the head with the palms or fists from the front of the head to the back. Pat to and fro about 20 times.

Pat the arms

Pat up and down the front, back and sides of the left arm with the right palm or fist 10 times on each side. Then pat the right arm with the left palm or fist in the same way.

Pat the shoulders

Pat the left shoulder with the right palm or fist and the right shoulder with the left palm or fist. Pat them alternatively for 10 times each.

Pat the back

Pat up and down the right side of the lower back with the left palm or fist, then the left side of the lower back with the right palm or fist for 20 times each side.

Figure 6: Patting the arms.

Pat the chest

Pat the left and right sides of the chest with the opposite palm or fist alternatively. Pat from the top to the bottom then the bottom to the top for 20 times on each side.

Pat the waist and abdomen

Taking the waist as an axis turn the upper body to the left then to the right. As you turn, pat the left side of the waist with the right palm or fist and the right side of the waist with the left palm or fist. Pat from top to bottom and move from the inside of the waist and abdomen outwards. Pat 20 times on each side.

Figure 7: Patting the legs.

Pat the buttocks

Pat the left buttocks with the left palm or fist and the right buttocks with the right palm or fist. Pat 20 times on each side.

Pat the legs

Sit on the floor with legs outstretched and knees slightly bent. Pat up and down the front, back and sides of the legs with both hands from the top of the leg downwards for 40 times each side.

To get the full benefit of this exercise it should be performed on a regular basis.

Having discussed the need to balance our work and exercise we'll now take a look at two other essential parts of our daily routine – rest and sleep.

Part Two
Rest and Sleep

ঔ৹

An intriguing study of 5,000 adults over a period of eight years found that those who slept for seven to eight hours a night had the lowest death rate for all causes of death including cancer, stroke, or heart disease. Remarkably it was found that short sleepers of six hours or less or very long sleepers who consistently slept for a lot more than nine hours were 30 per cent more likely to die prematurely.[9] The results of this study will not surprise those who practice Chinese medicine. During the night our Qi withdraws inside us and nourishes our organs. If we don't get enough rest and sleep we will not be replenishing our energy. In time we will be drawing on reserves and depleting ourselves.

Lynn didn't always get enough sleep:

> I used to be very much into the London life, working hard and going out and living it up – I was young and full of spirit. I got tired and didn't know why ... the London lifestyle was quite competitive – where you go, who you go with. I didn't get enough sleep but it was like an endurance test. I became ill because I was stressed out. Now I go to bed and sleep. I don't go out every night, I go out twice a week. I know I need to respect my body.

Jan is a hard worker but she always gets enough sleep:

> I sleep a lot. I always have at least eight hours rest. If I'm really busy it's the one thing I continue to do. I think it's really important – at least I have that time at night to recharge and rest and allow myself to get over what's gone on the day before. Rest makes me fresh again.

Although about eight hours of sleep is normal for us when we are well, when we are ill it is important for us to rest for longer. If our Qi has become weakened from ill-health, rest will replenish it.

Sometimes the best 'cure' for our illnesses is to go to bed and sleep until we are better. If we feel like sleeping for long periods this may be our body telling us that we need to rest in order to recover.

Our Posture when we Sleep

About one third of our life is spent sleeping. To enable us to get the greatest health benefits from sleeping it is important that we sleep in a good posture and are relaxed. Some Qigong practitioners suggest that we sleep on our back so that our spine is straight and our body is unconstricted.

Another traditional position is to lie on our right side with the top leg bent and the other leg straight. The right hand can be placed under the head for a pillow and the left hand rests on the thigh. In this position the heart is high up and does not get constricted and the liver, which the Chinese say 'stores Blood', is lower down and hence receives more blood. This posture also allows our Qi to circulate freely.

Figure 8: Correct sleeping position.

We should not use a pillow which is too high, as this will place our neck in a bad posture and constrict the blood flow to the head. This can cause neck problems, headaches and affect the eyesight.

The Midday Nap

Many Chinese people have a short rest during the day, after their lunch. This rest is usually for no longer than half an hour.

Studies confirm this to be beneficial. When people in a laboratory were allowed to sleep without restriction, an interesting pattern developed. They began to prefer to take a restful nap in the middle of the day. Although they didn't always sleep, the rest left them refreshed and ready for the afternoon. Research now suggests that an afternoon nap could be more in tune with our natural biological rhythms than just one long sleep at night.[10]

Mike, who rests during the day, told me:

I sleep after lunch when I'm working and it's important for me to get through the rest of the day. It gives me space between lunch and actual work. I've been doing it for years. If I didn't do it I'd feel the pressure of work more.

If I Have Difficulty Sleeping

There is nothing worse than tossing and turning and finding we are unable to sleep. The Chinese say that before sleeping we should 'first relax the heart'. This means that we should try not to go to bed excited, nervous or overstimulated. In order to help us sleep better, here are some suggestions:

1 Cultivate going to bed at a regular time each night – even if you don't immediately fall asleep.
2 Cut out caffeine-based stimulants such as coffee and tea. Buy decaffeinated drinks or drink herbal teas and water.
3 Don't engage in stimulating activities before bed. Watching television, reading exciting books or vigorous activity are all stimulating and keep us awake.

4   Don't eat late at night – you will go to bed still digesting your food.

5. Do a relaxation exercise – see the relaxation exercise below or buy a relaxation tape.

6. Meditate or do a gentle Qigong exercise before bed (*see Qigong Exercise before sleeping on page 106*).

7. Massage your feet, especially at the illustrated acupuncture point. Massaging this point helps to bring excess energy from the head to the feet, thus calming the Qi and helping us to sleep.

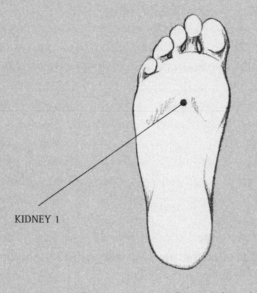

KIDNEY 1

Figure 9: Massage feet to induce sleep.

Consider whether your diet is deficient in 'Blood' nourishing food. If you are what the Chinese call 'Blood-deficient' you may feel unsettled inside, causing difficulty sleeping. For more on this see Chapter 2 and fill in the questionnaire 'Am I Blood-Deficient?' on page 215.

For more on insomnia see Chapter 7, page 180. If you have chronic insomnia and these suggestions don't help, visit a practitioner of Chinese medicine.

A Qigong Exercise before Sleeping

This 10-minute exercise can be performed while lying in bed and can help insomnia. It can also be done when we are ill and confined to bed.

1 Lie relaxed in bed on your back.
2 Hold the arms at right angles to the body with the elbows slightly bent. Keep the palms facing each other and the fingers slightly separated. The hands are about shoulder width apart.
3 Imagine holding a large soft ball between the hands.
4 A magnetic feeling of attraction and resistance will begin to develop between the palms. As the sensation builds, allow the hands to slowly move in and out. Breathe out as the palms move outwards and breathe in as the palms move inwards.
5 When practicing begin by using larger movements. Later move on to smaller movements. The smaller movements gradually develop a state of relaxation and tranquility.
6 After about 10 minutes a feeling of Qi should have developed between the palms. Place the palms on the Tan Tien. The Tan Tien is about one and a half inches below the navel (*see page 146*).

This exercise can also be performed at other times of the day, in a standing or sitting position. It will also help to develop our concentration and memory and develop our Qi flow between the hands.

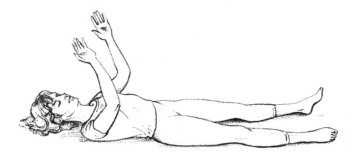

Figure 10: A Qigong exercise before sleeping.

Making Time for Rest and Relaxation

Relaxation is as important to our health as sleep. Life in the 21st century is becoming increasingly fast, making it difficult for many people to make time for rest. Sue who overworked realized when she became ill that she had to make space for herself. She told me:

> Since the breast cancer I pay much more attention to when I'm feeling tired. When I'm getting busier I now cut things out. I have to say 'no'. I also make sure that I sit down in the evening and go to bed at 10pm, read for half an hour, then get a good night's sleep.

For those of us who are always on the go, we might try Jan's ingenious way of making sure she gets time off:

> I used to plan work time and achieving work goals but found I didn't rest. In order to rest I now timetable in my relaxing time and time off. I also look at the balance of working days compared to rest days and make sure I have time for myself – especially as I do lots of weekend work. If I do this I can take time out and not worry about the fact that I'm not doing things.

Ways we can Rest and Relax

It is all too easy to get caught up with caring for others and never spending time nourishing ourselves. This is especially true of mothers with young children or carers. Booking in some space for pleasurable activity, even if it is only for a short time every week, can rejuvenate us.

There are many healthy ways of relaxing. Some suggestions are:

- listening to a relaxation tape
- going out for a gentle walk in the country
- meditating
- having a massage
- taking a relaxing bath.

Some of us prefer to relax inside our homes either by ourselves or with others. Others prefer to go out for relaxation. Relaxation can overlap with exercise and many people who do Qi exercises are pleased to find they are doing a relaxing activity which they also enjoy. Whatever we decide to do, it must be enjoyable. If it is not enjoyable it won't be relaxing. Relaxation inevitably has positive repercussions on our health.

Holidays are of course an important way of getting rest and relaxation. Sue, who spoke to us about overworking, now makes sure she rests and has a holiday every year. She says:

> Now every March to April I have a good holiday. This year I'm going to Turkey. I feel I need to do it and make sure it happens every year. It's self-regulating time out and it's good for me.

A Simple Relaxation Exercise

Here is a relaxation exercise which can be useful to rest us in the middle of the day or to prepare us for a relaxing sleep before bed.[11]

1 Sit with the back straight or lie down with the arms and legs outstretched and the head raised on a low pillow.
2 Relax the body down three lines:
   a. **Line 1** – down the two sides – the outer sides of the head – neck – shoulders – upper arms – elbows – wrists – palms – fingers.
   b. **Line 2** – top of the head – face – neck – chest – abdomen – thighs – knees – legs – ankles – toes.
   c. **Line 3** – head – back of the neck – back – waist – back of thighs – hollows of the knees – back of the legs – heels – soles of feet.

Each line will take from one to five minutes to complete. Having completed the three lines focus your attention on to the lower abdomen for about one minute. Repeat the exercise as many times as you wish.

Resting after Pregnancy

Rest is particularly important immediately after giving birth. At this time a woman in China is said to 'be in the month'. During this period she rests completely. All her needs are taken care of – traditionally by her mother-in-law. As well as resting she eats plenty of meat, especially chicken, to strengthen her, avoids getting emotionally upset, and as she has been temporarily weakened by the process of giving birth, she also avoids the effects of Wind and Cold (*see Chapter 6*).

'Doing the month' and our health

In a study of over 100 Chinese-American women in California, those who were questioned said they considered 'doing the month' was beneficial to their health. Most thought women who don't rest after giving birth would suffer 'grave consequences' for their health later on. These might be illnesses such as poor energy, joint problems, infections and depression.

'Doing the month' and post-natal depression

Interestingly, women who 'do the month' don't expect to get post-natal depression. The concept of it didn't make sense to the Chinese-American women questioned. This is in contrast to women in Western countries who often take it for granted that they will suffer from depression after childbirth.

A period of rest after giving birth used to be a normal part of Western post-natal treatment. Nowadays many women in the West no longer regard this as necessary. Women often leave hospital soon after having a baby and although their energy is still depleted they go back to 'normal' life almost immediately. Interestingly, Chinese tradition states that if a woman does not 'do the month' and subsequently becomes ill there is only one way she can restore her health – to become pregnant again and this time to 'do the month' properly.[12]

Summary

1 Many people are now in the habit of overworking. Sometimes taking proper lunch breaks and finding time for more rest is enough to counteract this.

2 If we are ill we need to convalesce fully to avoid ill-health in the future.

3 We need both 'Internal' and 'External' exercise to stay fit. It is best to exercise regularly and if possible to incorporate it into our daily work routine – especially if our lifestyle is very static. We can do physical exercise at least three times a week for 20–30 minutes. Alongside, or as an alternative to, physical exercise a gentler Qigong exercise routine carried out every day will increase our health and well-being.

4 To protect our health we need around eight hours sleep a night. Our posture and the quality of the sleep we get are important. A midday rest can be a great energy booster for us. If we have difficulty sleeping, cutting out stimulants and late night meals and adding relaxing activities before bed can support us.

5 Relaxation time is important. If we are overworked we can say 'no' to things we might do. If necessary we can plan rest time into our life. Relaxation exercises can help to relax us.

6 Chinese women take one month's rest after giving birth to fully recover. This is called 'doing the month'.

The Secret of Protecting Ourselves from the Environment

Most Chinese people understand that they need to protect themselves from the environment. At one time most mothers and mothers-in-law in the West also knew this secret, as Chris's story illustrates.

Chris has two children, Maggie aged four and Emma aged two. She enjoys being a mother. Life was very different for her six years ago when she was desperate to have children and couldn't conceive. Here she recalls what happened:

> I went for acupuncture because I wanted to get pregnant. I'd miscarried one year before and had been unable to conceive since. Cold was something we talked about a lot while I was having the treatment and I could feel a cold center in my belly. My acupuncturist would warm my tummy by heating a special herb called 'moxa' on it and I would also do this at home. I also cut out Cold food from my diet. Later on I left my job as a social worker which made my life less stressful.
>
> It was quite a time into treatment before my practitioner found out that I didn't wear slippers and walked around the house with bare feet. When she realized, she nearly fell off her chair! My response was, 'Oh no, my mother-in-law was right!'
>
> My mother-in law used to say, 'You'll suffer. That cold will travel up your legs.' I hadn't believed her. I'd always had cold feet and the floors of my house were made of stone. When my practitioner told me to wear slippers I did, as it was obviously important. I realize that the Cold had affected my

tummy and made it hard for me to conceive. My feet began to warm up and not long after I got pregnant.

Slippers are now really important in this house. My own feet are now warm. I always wear slippers and so do my children. I get really concerned when I see other people's children without them as I've experienced the consequences of not wearing something on my feet.

Wearing shoes and keeping the feet warm can prevent Cold traveling up to the lower abdomen and causing infertility. Cold can cause other problems too and we'll be discussing them later in the chapter. Chinese people have retained this knowledge about the climate, whilst people born after the Second World War in the West seem to have ignored or lost it. Many other useful recommendations have been discarded as 'old wives' tales'.

In this chapter we will have the opportunity to rediscover many other simple 'health rules' that have been temporarily lost. First let's examine some other 'old wives' tales'.

Old Wives' Tales in the West

When I was young I remember being told various 'old wives' tales' to help me to look after my health. My mother knew them well. So did most of my school teachers and even my friends. Like me, most of my friends chose to ignore much of the advice that we were given.

The following are some common 'old wives' tales' that I remember:

- don't sit on wet grass
- don't sit on stone steps
- change out of wet clothes
- don't sleep with your head facing a fire or radiator
- dry your washed hair before going out
- don't swim during your period
- always wear a hat when it's cold
- don't go to sleep with wet hair

- cover your neck in the wind
- avoid sitting or sleeping in a draught
- don't wash your hair during a period
- air your clothes before wearing them
- don't sit in the midday sun
- don't walk around without shoes on
- add or take off extra clothes when you change from a warm to cold environment
- don't leave your back or abdomen uncovered
- don't make love during a period
- when traveling home from abroad wrap up warmly for when the temperature drops
- don't sit on hot radiators
- dry yourself thoroughly after bathing
- don't swim when you have a cold
- wear a vest.

The list is endless and you will probably be able to think of many more.

Why did I disregard this advice? Because until I learned Chinese medicine the implications of ignoring these sensible warnings were meaningless to me. All of the above advice is about the effects of what the Chinese call Wind, Cold, Damp, Dryness and Heat. These different climatic conditions and temperatures are known to practitioners of Chinese medicine as the climatic or 'External' causes of disease.

Why are the Climatic Causes Important?

Throughout history the Chinese have understood that there is both an Internal and an External 'climate' which can affect our health. In Chapter 3 we talked about the Internal climate – our emotions.

The External 'climates' can have equally powerful consequences on our health as our emotions, if we do not learn to protect ourselves from them. We often instinctively know the influence they are having on us. Wind can make us vulnerable to colds and flu, Damp can make us extremely sluggish, tired and depressed, Cold can create intense pain and Heat can make us irritable. However, these are only a few of the many symptoms attributable to the climate.

We'll discover more about the effects of different climatic conditions as we go through this chapter. These will include how the Chinese view each of the 'climates', the signs and symptoms which they can generate and how we can protect ourselves from them.

In Part 1 we will discuss Cold and Wind and in Part 2 we'll look at Damp, Dryness and Heat.

Part One
Cold and Wind

Cold

Earlier, Chris told us about the effects of Cold traveling up her legs to her lower abdomen and how this stopped her from conceiving. Cold can cause many other symptoms, often without our realizing it. These can include period pains, joint pains, stomach upsets, abdominal pains, back pains, diarrhea, cold hands and feet and circulation problems. When we 'catch' a cold the Chinese say that this is a combination of Wind with Cold. We will discuss Wind later (*see page 119*).

A common symptom of Cold is pain.

Pain and Cold

When the temperature is cold it makes things slow down and contract. We can contrast this with heat which speeds things up and makes them more expansive. If on a snowy day we make a snowball and hold it in our hand for too long then our fingers will start to hurt. This pain is due to the tissues contracting. If we eat ice cream too quickly it can get stuck in our gullet and cause severe pain until it passes down into our stomach. The pain from Cold is sharp and intense. Here is how Cold affected Linda:

> At one time I lived in an old building with large windows which didn't fit. It was really cold in the winter. I went into heavy-duty depression. I began to have pains all over my body and I'd wake up feeling scared by the whole thing. I also had chilblains which were very bad. I was so cold that it was unbearable. It got to the stage that wearing more clothes didn't work. I'd no idea why I was getting so ill and that being in that environment was affecting me until I went to see a practitioner of Chinese medicine. She told me the Cold had got into my system.

Other signs and symptoms of Cold

As well as pain there are other symptoms of Cold which affect us. These include feeling chilly or disliking Cold, a preference for warmth, loose stools, watery discharges or profuse urination.

Ann tells us about how she was affected by Cold:

> I've always had a tendency to be a chilly person. If I go near the refrigerator in the supermarket I immediately want to go to pee. If I go out in the cold weather I have to wrap up warmly otherwise I'll get painful hands, feet and ears. A number of years ago I got period pains. I was learning a martial art and practicing three times a week. We practiced without shoes. In the winter the room was unheated and the mat was very cold. It took me a long time to realize that the Cold was affecting me and giving me period pains. I got special dispensation to cover my feet when it was very cold.

Which parts of the body are affected by Cold?

Cold can affect various parts of our bodies. When we sit on cold seats it can affect our lower abdomen in the same way as it does through our feet. When we leave our abdomen exposed to the Cold it can affect our back or stomach, giving us pain or a cold feeling in the area. If we leave our chest uncovered, Cold may travel inwards to affect our chest and if we leave various joints exposed it may cause our tissues to contract and give us joint pain. If we eat

Cold food it may also affect our stomach and lower abdomen. Here Claire and Jenny tell us of their experiences.

Claire said:

> If I sit on cold metal seats the Cold and Damp can affect me. I was recently thinking of writing to British Rail about the seats on station platforms. We used to have such lovely wooden seats and they were warm and easy to sit on if you were tired. Now they've changed their seats to metal ones. Within a short time of sitting on them I feel uncomfortable and disturbed as the Cold is coming up into my abdomen.

Jenny has noticed:

> I always wear a long vest unless it's boiling weather. If my lower back isn't covered I'll feel very cold. In the winter I wear long and short sleeved vests over the top of each other. I've also noticed that if I get very cold feet I can get symptoms of sciatica up the sides of my legs. It only lasts a day but I'm aware that I have to be careful.

Who is affected by Cold?

The winter of 1963 was one of the coldest in France since the beginning of the century. In that year the mortality of people over the age of 60 increased by 15.7 per cent compared to the previous winter.[1] The cold weather puts extra stress on the organs of those who are already ill. There are more strokes, heart attacks and respiratory infections in the winter. Even the incidence of deaths from illnesses such as cirrhosis of the liver, diabetes and cancer is increased. Old and frail people are the most susceptible to Cold and other climatic conditions as their Qi is weaker.

Some of us don't notice the cold at all whilst others have a greater tendency to feel chilly. Those of us who are always sitting close to fires and radiators and who love holidays in sunny climates are probably more affected by the cold. Some people ignore the fact that they feel cold but still need to protect themselves from it. The more we are effected by the cold, the more it can affect our health. Patricia told me:

> I hate the cold and I feel it a lot in the winter. I have to wrap up really
> warmly to protect myself. My husband on the other hand is never really
> bothered by the cold. He notices damp weather though and can feel quite
> ill when it's very damp. Damp never bothers me.

Cold will affect those who are vulnerable to it but will also affect those people who are unavoidably caught in it for a long time. Daphne is an example:

> A couple of years ago I went to look at a house I was going to buy. I had to
> wait for someone in the house for half the day. By 5pm it was dark and I'd
> got cold. I walked around trying to get warm but was still cold. The next day
> I had diarrhea for the day and it clicked that I'd got chilled in my stomach
> from the Cold and Damp.

Other warnings against the Cold come in the form of some of the old wives' tales we've already mentioned.

Cold and the uterus

Two of those famous old wives' tales are 'don't make love during your period' and 'don't swim during your period'. During the time women are menstruating the Chinese have noted that our uterus is more vulnerable to the effects of the elements.

Since the coming of tampons many of us who didn't swim during our periods feel free enough to throw this sound advice to the wind (or maybe we should say to the cold as well!) The uterus is very sensitive to the Cold when we are having our periods and once Cold has entered the uterus it can cause period pains, scanty periods, or possibly even infertility.

Cold food

Finally, it is important to mention the effects of Cold food on the digestive system. The Chinese have understood that many health problems can be caused by eating too much Cold food. For more about this turn back to page 34.

Protecting ourselves from the Cold

Some time ago a politician in England advised old people to wear long johns and woolly hats when it was cold. She was laughed at by many for her old fashioned and tactless advice. Leaving aside the politics and the context in which the advice was given, her advice was in fact very sound. Long johns and hats are a sensible choice for many of us.

Here is a summary of methods we can adopt to protect ourselves from the Cold:

1   Wear many layers of clothes in winter. The layers trap warmth and protect us better than only one thickness. Clothes can include thermal vests and long underwear, a thick jacket, long coats past the knee and more than one jumper.

2   Feeling sharp pains when you are out in cold weather is a sign that an area is affected by the Cold. This can be painful ears, hands, feet or head. If you feel these warning signs, cover up. Heat is easily lost from the extremities by people of all ages – it can be important to wear gloves and hats as well as warm shoes and socks. Those old wives' tales which tell us, 'always wear a hat when it's cold' and 'don't walk around without shoes on' give us really sensible advice.

3   Don't sit on cold metal seats or stone steps without insulation. You can protect yourself by sitting on a newspaper or magazine or even carrying a blow up cushion. It may be better to stand if there is nothing else available. This especially applies to people who have sensitivity to Cold including women who have a tendency to get period pains from Cold in the uterus.

4   Be aware of your constitution – if you are a naturally chilly person, Cold will have a greater effect than if you are more warm-blooded. Older people are particularly vulnerable to the Cold. Also be aware of the seasons – when the weather is hot we can wear fewer clothes, swim in cold water or eat Colder food.

5   Cold food (*see page 35*) can give us stomach pain especially if we eat it in vast quantities or we have a tendency to feel the Cold. When it's cold

it's important to eat hotter food and keep warm. If you *do* get stomach pains from the Cold, immediately put something warm, such as a hot water bottle, on the area.

6   Heat your environment adequately. It is preferable to keep just one room well-heated than to live in a Cold house. Linda who talked to us earlier (*see page 115*) suffered the consequences of living in a Cold house when she became ill and depressed.

7   Avoid leaving the torso uncovered even if it is fashionable to do so. Even in mild weather we can get Cold 'invading' the abdomen or back. This can cause stomach, bowel, or back problems and even period pains or infertility. We also need to cover our legs. People who wear miniskirts in the cold put more subcutaneous fat on their thighs to protect them. Wearing thicker tights or even two layers of tights will prevent this – the longer the skirt the thinner the legs!

Having looked closely at the effects of Cold on the body we'll now go on to something the Chinese call 'Wind'. Unlike Cold, Wind is something which has never been fully described in the West in relation to our health.

Wind

Wind in the body is like wind in nature. Any illness which arises suddenly, comes and goes rapidly and goes through many swift changes is described as 'Wind' by the Chinese. Most conditions of Wind are also located in the top part of the body and at the surface.

Signs and symptoms of Wind

The most notable symptoms of Wind are infections such as the common cold or influenza. Acute infections such as colds or flu arise out of the blue, change rapidly and are often located in the head.

Here Dave describes his 'Wind-Cold':

I felt fine the night before. In the middle of the night I woke up with a sore throat and knew I was in for an infection. The next day I felt terrible. My nose was running, my jaw ached, my eyes hurt and I felt extremely tired and shivery. Two days later all my symptoms had gone during the day, yet I still woke up coughing at night. It was five days before it went completely.

Other symptoms of Wind could be joint pains which move around or come and go (as opposed to pain from Cold which is a contracting pain). Symptoms that come on suddenly such as neck pains, facial paralysis, sudden severe dizziness. Some acute headaches can also be due to Wind.

Wind as the 'spearhead' of disease

In Chinese medicine Wind is termed 'the spearhead of disease'. The Chinese also say that Wind can be the means by which Cold, Heat, Damp and Dryness are driven into the body. We can compare this with the 'wind-chill factor' which we often hear mentioned on the weather forecast. Wind-chill describes how a strong wind exaggerates our experience of Cold. Put in another way, we could say that the higher the wind-chill factor, the more Cold is being driven into the body.

Most acute infections are caused by a mixture of elements, with Wind as a spearhead driving in another climatic cause. We mentioned earlier that the common cold is called Wind-Cold and is a mixture of Wind with Cold in the body. Infections which involve a high temperature or a red sore throat would be called Wind-Heat. Many joint problems are a mixture of Wind, Cold and Damp. We will be finding out more about the effects of Damp later in the chapter.

Our susceptibility to Wind

There are two main ways that we can be affected by Wind.

1 Being caught in the 'windy' conditions – the word 'windy' can include any of the following:
    • a windy day
    • a draught
    • the breeze from a fan
    • air conditioning in homes, cars or buildings.

2   Sudden weather changes. A sudden change can include:
- any out of season change in the weather
- coming home from a holiday abroad
- moving in and out of shops and other centrally heated or air conditioned buildings.

The effects of changing temperatures

Research carried out as far back as the late 1950s provided some insight into the effects of changes in the weather on our health. Two researchers, Dr W. Feige and Dr R. Freund, were able to establish that many rheumatic attacks which were severe enough for a person to stop work were often related to changes in the weather. Over a period of two years they followed a group of 35 out-patients with rheumatic symptoms. Interestingly their findings were that, 'The most harmful meteorological events are a sudden drop in temperature, strong winds and the influx of polar air masses.' [2]

Another researcher called Laqueur observed that all forms of rheumatic disease are more common in Turkey than many other countries. In Turkey the summers are very hot and the winters are very cold. This is especially true in the capital, Ankara, where the temperature is very extreme. In comparison, the incidence of rheumatic problems is low in areas around the equator. Here the heat is constant and there is little difference between summer and winter.[3]

The effect of draughts, fans and windy weather

As well as changes in temperature, many people recognize that draughts, fans or windy weather make them ill. Terri has noticed that covering her neck prevents her from catching colds:

> I'm very sensitive to draughts and wind in both the winter and the summer.
> I never go out without a scarf especially if I'm a bit tired. I know I'll easily get
> a cold if there's wind around and I don't wear something around my neck.

Patsy now avoids sleeping in draughts:

Once when the weather was extremely hot I went to sleep with the fan on to keep me cool. The next day I had a terrible stiff neck. It was quite a while later that I realized that it had been caused by the fan creating a draught.

Don't colds come from germs?

Chinese doctors discovered that droplet infection could cause colds as far back as the Qing dynasty around AD 1700. Doctors realized that knowing about germs did not protect us from illness – there will always be germs around that we can 'catch'. What protects us from infections is keeping our immune system strong. When we are trying to adjust to changes in climate or other causes of 'Wind', our immune system is weakened and we are more vulnerable to infection.

In reality we don't always know the actual events which led up to us 'catching' a cold. Sometimes we remember getting chilled, being caught in windy conditions or being affected by weather changes and sometimes we don't. It doesn't matter. To the Chinese, having the symptoms of a climatic factor is enough for it to be there. Like Paul, we may be getting a 'Wind-Cold' but don't know why. He told me:

There have been a few instances when I thought I was going to get a cold and had aversion to Cold. I didn't always know why I was getting it. The cold was at its very beginning stages and I nipped it in the bud by having a very hot bath then going to bed wrapped up warmly so that I could sweat it out.

If we protect ourselves from these climatic conditions we will keep healthier and be less susceptible to the germs which cause a cold.

Protecting ourselves from the Wind

Here are some of the many ways we can protect ourselves from Wind.

1   Cover your neck and head in the wind to prevent colds, flu and stiff necks. Wind can also affect our joints if we don't protect ourselves. In this case it will cause pain which moves from place to place.

2 Take care in changing temperatures. Add or take away clothes. This is especially necessary when we are returning from sunny holidays abroad to a cold climate or when moving in and out of heated shops in the cold weather.

3 Avoid draughts of any kind – especially sleeping in a draught or sitting or standing directly in front of a fan. Also take care to wear enough clothes to protect yourself when you are in air conditioned environments.

4 Avoid exercising in the Wind. This is important if you become hot when exercising and your pores open. The Wind can easily 'invade' through the pores making us susceptible to catching an infection.

5 If we are feeling tired, shocked, emotionally upset or are 'under the weather' in any way we should be extra vigilant about protecting ourselves from the 'Wind'. Our immune system may be weakened making us more susceptible.

6 Wind and Cold can easily combine, so any of the suggestions for protecting ourselves from Cold also apply to some extent to protection from the Wind. Wearing gloves, hats and warm footwear are all important steps in protecting ourselves from infections.

In Part 2 we will discuss the three other climatic causes which are Damp, Dryness and Heat. We will also look at how the climatic causes can combine together.

Part Two
Damp, Dryness and Heat

Have you ever been out on a damp or humid day and felt heavy-limbed, achy, lethargic and a bit depressed? Then as soon as the day brightened up you felt better? If so, you may be susceptible to the effects of Damp. Some are more vulnerable to it than others. Pat tells us:

One of the things about Damp is the awareness I have of it – other people aren't always as aware of it as I am. I can smell it and feel it and it affects me strongly. If it's been raining for a long time I get stiffer in my body and my hips ache.

Pat was very aware of Damp and hence was extremely affected by it. In general, the climates we are most sensitive to will have the most negative effect on our health. Other people will be less affected by a Damp environment and more by other climates. Earlier Pauline told us that she hated the Cold and wasn't affected by Damp. Her husband was the opposite – he didn't mind the Cold weather but disliked Damp.

Damp

Living in a damp country can be enough to affect our health to some degree. Great Britain is a very damp country, with Wales and Ireland being particularly problematic.

Damp conditions which can affect us

As well as living in a Damp country or environment, we can be affected by these kinds of Damp conditions:

1 frequently being in or near water
2 living in a Damp house
3 wearing damp clothes
4 sitting on damp grass
5 not drying ourselves properly.

Here are some examples of the various ways that Damp can affect us. Graham has noticed the Damp in his environment:

I used to work on a trout farm which was situated at the bottom of a valley on top of a spring. The whole atmosphere was Damp. I also lived in a Damp house with thick stone walls and inadequate heating. No one used to talk to me for one and a half hours after I got up as I was so obnoxious and I could only do routine things. After one and a half hours I could start to be civil. I became very run down and after work I would lie about as I felt totally lethargic.

Delia was affected in her hands:

Last year I went back to Ireland every weekend for a while to spring clean my parents' house. I spent a lot of the time with my hands covered in rubber gloves in buckets of water. After a while my hands started aching and I realized it was the water. It was as if I had had my hands in damp plastic bags all the time. My hands were stiff and achy in the muscles and fingers. It stayed for a few weeks then gradually went.

Chris had symptoms of Damp after getting soaked in the rain:

Last year I got soaked with the wind and wet having to rush out and fasten down doors in a storm. My head got extremely wet. I loved the feeling of getting soaked and I was invigorated by it at the time. After a couple of days though I couldn't think. It was as if I had a 'Damp' brain – it felt like cotton wool in there and I was completely muzzy.

These are only a few examples, so let's hear more about how Damp can affect our health.

The symptoms of Damp

If we dislike damp weather, as Sheila told us she did earlier, this may indicate that we are vulnerable to the Damp. Feeling achy is a symptom which may signal that Damp has penetrated our joints – Delia, for example, got achy hands from immersing them in water. Another common symptom of Damp is a muzzy head such as the one described by Chris after she was soaked in the wind and rain.

Chinese medicine describes Damp as heavy, sticky and lingering. Graham described feeling very lethargic and wanting to lie about in the evenings. The lethargy and tiredness which comes from Damp is often described by people as a heavy feeling combined with a desire to lie down a lot. I was once told by a patient, 'I lie down and feel like I'm wearing a cloak which is made of lead.'

Other symptoms include feeling heavy-limbed, a lack of concentration, a stuffy feeling in the chest or abdomen, oozing discharges or loose stools. The movement of Damp is downwards and it is heavy and lingering. This is in contrast to Wind which travels upwards, changes quickly and is easier to move. Damp tends to be the hardest climatic cause of disease to clear from our system.

Drying ourselves thoroughly

Two old wives' tales are 'dry your washed hair before going out', and 'don't go to sleep with wet hair'. If we do this we can become more vulnerable to Wind and Cold as well as Damp. Eleanor learnt about sleeping with wet hair the hard way:

> One thing I'd always been told when I was young was not to go out with wet hair. In my teens I hit on the idea that I would bathe and wash my hair at night, place a towel on my pillow and in the morning I then had dry hair. I remember feeling smug about the other girls who went out with wet hair. I never really thought much else about what I was doing or why I shouldn't go out with wet hair. With hindsight it enhanced my propensity to colds and lung infections. At that time I was getting a lot of colds. Although I did it less over the years it was only when I was 31 that I stopped when I learnt about Chinese medicine. I'm much more careful of my health in every way now.

Some old wives' tales also speak of other ways of protecting ourselves from the Damp. They include, 'don't sit on wet grass' and 'dry yourself thoroughly after bathing'. If we don't do these things we can become more susceptible to any of the symptoms of Damp.

Diet and Damp

Some foods are said to be more Phlegm and Damp-forming than others. These tend to be 'sticky' foods such as dairy produce, bananas, peanuts and greasy food. Eating too much of these foods will increase the amount of Damp in the body. For more on Damp-forming foods turn to pages 22–23.

Protecting ourselves from Damp

Damp is very penetrating so it is essential to protect ourselves from it. Here are a few suggestions:

1   Make sure your environment is dry. If you live in a Damp house a good damp-proof course may be the answer. If you live in surroundings that can't be dried out it may be best to move. Sometimes it is impossible to move – as a temporary measure, place a de-humidifier in the house.
2   Keep your body dry and protected from Damp. Do this by never going out or sleeping with wet hair, drying yourself thoroughly and not sitting in damp places.
3   Wear dry clothes. Our grannies in their wisdom would always insist on airing their clothes in an airing cupboard and also 'changing out of wet clothes'. This removed any remaining dampness from them and prevented rheumatic problems.
4   If your clothes are damp because you've been sweating make sure you change them – but not until you have finished sweating. If you change your clothes while still sweating your pores will be open. In this case Damp and Cold can easily get in and you can catch a chill or get joint problems.
5   If you are vulnerable to Damp, be careful about the food you eat and avoid the Phlegm and Damp-forming foods mentioned above.
6   Some people are more susceptible to Damp than others. If you feel heavy, achy and lethargic in a Damp climate you will be helped by all of the above advice.

The opposite of Damp is Dryness.

Dryness

Dryness as a cause of disease is seen less in many parts of the West than Cold, Wind and Damp. This doesn't mean that we aren't affected by it.

Charles, for example, once lived in a very Dry house:

> I once lived in a shared house which had central heating – it was double glazed, well insulated and had no draughts at all – it was almost hermetically sealed. I began to get a dry throat and a hoarse voice most of the time. The others had similar symptoms and we didn't realize why. I could feel my skin drying out after half an hour of being in the house. The people in the house had colds and flu a lot. In the end I realized what was happening and got a humidifier. It reduced its effect on us.

Signs and symptoms of Dryness

The main symptoms of Dryness are not surprisingly dry symptoms – a dry nose, dry throat, dry eyes, dry mouth, dry skin or a dry cough with little sputum.

Who gets affected by Dryness?

Those typically affected by Dryness are people like Charles who work in dry, centrally heated environments or live in very Dry houses. Just as Great Britain is a Damp country, other countries can be very Dry. Here Janice remembers getting ill on a visit to China:

> I remember stepping outside in Beijing and breathing in. I had the extraordinary feeling of the Cold and Dryness going through my nose and deep into my lungs. A few days later it turned into an infection. It was unlike anything I'd experienced before. I had a feeling of incredible dryness in my

lungs and an aching feeling in my chest. I had a hacking cough but no matter how much I coughed I just couldn't produce anything.

Protecting ourselves from Dryness

Living and working in a dry environment can be very debilitating and leave us exposed to getting symptoms of Dryness. Here are some simple means of combating Dryness:

1   Place a bowl of water in the room. Many people hang containers of water from a radiator. A more sophisticated method of dealing with dryness is to get a humidifier as Charles did.
2   If you are suffering from a dry cough or infection, breathing in steam from a bowl of hot water or breathing vapor into the lungs will help to bring moisture to the throat and chest. Vaporizers can be bought from an old-fashioned chemist and some health food shops.
3   The atmosphere of a plane can be very drying. When flying drink lots of water to make sure you don't dehydrate.

Heat

After a long, cold winter the sun brings us out of our houses and we become more active and sociable. Our bodies are better equipped to deal with Heat than with Cold. When we are warm, the blood vessels at the skin dilate and allow the heat to escape. We also perspire. As the perspiration evaporates we cool down.

If, however, we are exposed to the Heat for long periods we will quickly become ill. People who work in hot laundries or bakeries can suffer the impact of Heat as well as those who are affected by the sun.

Signs and symptoms of Heat

Symptoms of prolonged exposure are irritability, high fever, cramps, rapid breathing and palpitations. If this becomes extreme it will become serious. Our temperature will rise and we will get dehydrated. Later we can go into shock and heart failure.

Now that scientists have discovered holes in the ozone layer and there is an increase in the incidence of skin cancer, ways of protecting ourselves from the heat and sun are well documented. Most people who holiday frequently or live in hot countries are well aware of the effects of the sun.

The effects of the sun

Daphne tells us how she learned to look after herself in South Africa:

> I'm aware that we can have too much heat. I grew up in South Africa where it was very hot. My father instilled in us from an early age that we should 'treat the sun with respect'. This was even before there were holes in the ozone layer. In South Africa you could get burnt in a flash. I don't overexpose myself in the heat and dryness as the heat dries the skin.

Simon also lived in a hot country:

> Between the ages of 15 and 45 I lived in Ontario and I used to go road running. I was out in the heat for prolonged periods. Often the climate would beat me more than anything else. I would get dehydrated. I now recognize the signs by a feeling of weakness down the backs of my arms and legs and a feeling that I'd have to drag myself or I would have succumbed to the fluid loss. It was a horrible feeling.

Until the 1920s people in the West didn't sunbathe much. It was fashionable to remain pale. Then Coco Chanel of the Chanel fashion house went on a cruise and came back with a suntan. A new craze for suntans was born and everyone wanted one. All of us sun worshippers who once laid in the sun for hours now know that we need to take extra care to avoid the worst effects of the sun.

Protecting ourselves from the Heat

1 Not staying out in the sun for long periods, protecting our skin with high factor sun creams and making sure we drink enough liquids are

important ways to shield ourselves from the effects of the sun.

2   If we like to sunbathe it is best to build up slowly and not to stay out – like mad dogs and Englishmen – in the midday sun.

3   Diet can also generate heat in the body. Heating foods include meats such as lamb and beef and hot curries. For more on heating food turn to pages 34–36.

We can also consider the way people who live in hot climates look after themselves.

4   Many people living in hot countries take a short siesta after their lunch. They know that it's best to avoid going out in the sun when it's at its hottest. After their siesta they wake up refreshed and can enjoy themselves well into the evening.

5   People who are indigenous to a hot country will also wear clothes which protect them from the sun. Often a shirt or blouse with sleeves is a better choice than a sleeveless top as this protects the shoulders. Wearing a hat will protect the skin on the face and head. Most of us are now aware that nothing ages our skin faster than too much sun which dries up the skin on the face.

Other Effects of Heat

External heat can make us ill but heat can also be generated internally. Chinese medicine notes that overwork or unresolved emotions can generate heat in our systems. During menopause many women get hot flushes. This heat is internally generated. It is due to the decline of the moistening and cooling Yin aspects of the body at this time of life. For more on menopause and overworking turn to Chapter 4. For lifestyle advice about hot flushes see pages 186–187. For more on the emotions see pages 61–78.

Climatic Factors Combining Together

We have touched on the fact that these climatic conditions don't affect us in isolation. When we examine the External climate in many countries we can understand that Wind, Cold, Damp, Dryness and Heat often combine. Some places are Cold and Damp, others Cold and Dry. Some areas are Hot and Humid while others are Hot and Dry. Earlier we talked about how Wind is the spearhead of disease and how it can drive the other climatic conditions into the body (*see page 120*).

Pain and Wind, Cold and Damp

Joint pains tend to be a combination of Wind, Cold and Damp. Wind causes moving pains, Cold causes intense, sharp pains and Damp causes aching and stiffness. A Chinese saying is that 'any stagnation can turn to heat'. When Wind, Cold and Damp remain stagnating in the joints for a period of time the joints may get hotter then become red and painful. Over a period of time nodules can then form on the joints. Chinese medicine teaches that this is due to the heat drying up the fluids in the joints. For more on joint pains see page 183.

Damp and Heat

Two climatic conditions which often combine together are Damp and Heat. These two combine easily when we live in humid conditions and we can also be affected by eating too much heating and damp-forming foods. The symptoms of Damp-Heat are comparable to what we in the West call infections – dirty, foul-smelling discharges, inflammation and swollen, inflamed joints. If we are aware of being susceptible to the effects of Damp and Heat we can try to protect ourselves from humid conditions and avoid eating Heating and Damp-forming foods.

Keeping Healthy with the Seasons

Some countries have huge seasonal variations in temperature while others have less changeable climates. We can adjust our lifestyles as the seasons vary. If we look at animals we notice that they change from season to season.

Animals adapt to winter temperatures by growing thick protective coats or hibernating. In a similar way we need to wear thicker clothes at this time of year. The Chinese note that in winter, when it is darker and colder, we should go to bed earlier, get up later and be less active.

In summer the animals lose their winter coats and are at their most energetic. In general we too are more active in summer and can go to bed later and rise earlier.

In spring the climate is more changeable and we can protect ourselves against wind and rain. There is an old saying which is 'N'er cast a clout till May is out.' This means don't cast off your warm clothes until May has gone. Whether 'May' is the month of May or the May blossoms we don't know but it is still useful advice. In autumn, of course, we should take care to add more layers of clothes as the weather gets colder.

Diet, Work, Rest, Exercise and Keeping Healthy

The healthier we are, the less we are affected by the elements. This can be achieved by balancing our diet, emotions, work, rest and exercise as well as looking after our constitution.

Food and water are becoming increasingly polluted (in Chapter 2 we discussed the purity of our food). The air is also becoming more polluted by traffic fumes, especially in urban areas. Spending more time in an environment which has clean air can be very restorative to our health. This can just be a walk in the countryside or by a river. Sadly the days are long gone when doctors sent their patients to the seaside to convalesce or when patients with tuberculosis were sent to the mountains to breathe fresh air. A healthy atmosphere and restful conditions are very healing.

If you wish to find out more about your susceptibility to the different climates turn to pages 212–216 and fill in the questionnaire about Cold, Wind, Damp, Dryness and Heat.

Summary

1   Climatic conditions are Cold, Wind, Damp, Dryness and Heat. They can affect us singly or in combination. Each of us is susceptible to different climatic conditions depending on our underlying constitution.

2   Cold can enter the body through our feet, our lower abdomen and back, our chest or our joints. Some of the main symptoms of Cold are intense, sharp pains, feeling chilly and disliking cold, profuse pale urination and

thin watery discharges. Eating too much Cold food can also affect our digestive system. We can protect ourselves from Cold by covering our feet and wearing other warm clothes.

3 Wind affects the top part of our body and includes symptoms which arise quickly, change rapidly and move location. These can include colds and other infections, stiff necks and facial paralysis. Wind includes a change in the temperature or 'windy' conditions including fans, draughts and air conditioning. We should be careful to protect our neck in the wind or to wrap up when we move between different environments.

4 Damp is heavy, sticky and lingering and will create symptoms of extreme lethargy, heavy limbs, stiff achy joints, lack of concentration, a stuffy chest or abdomen or even depression. Avoid Damp by changing out of wet clothes and living in dry conditions.

5 Dryness is rare in many parts of the West but we can get it from centrally heated offices, houses or planes. Symptoms of Dryness include a dry throat, hoarse voice, dry skin, dry nose or dry mouth. Place a bowl of water in a dry room to moisten the atmosphere.

6 Heat can cause irritation, dehydration, high fever, cramps, rapid breathing and palpitations. We can be affected by working in hot environments such as bakeries or laundries as well as staying out in the hot sun. People who are indigenous to a hot climate can teach us a great deal about respecting the heat. Heat can also be generated internally by overwork, emotions and eating too much heating food. During menopause, women's cooling Yin energy becomes depleted. This causes women to becoming hotter and drier causing hot flushes.

7 We can adapt our way of life and the clothes we wear to the seasons as the temperature changes.

The Secret of Respecting
Our Constitution

Have you ever wondered why some lucky people seem to avoid ill-health, whereas others easily succumb to any illnesses around? The answer lies in what is probably the best kept secret of all – our constitutional energy. To find out more we need to discover more about what the Chinese call our 'Jing'.

What is Jing?

Jing is constitutional energy which we inherit from our parents. It is often translated as 'essence' and it could also be called the primal substance from which we are made. While we are in the womb we are sustained by Jing. Once we are born, however, we are nourished by Qi energy which comes from the food we eat and the air we breathe. For more on Qi see pages 4 and 230.

Jing and our development

Although after our birth we are maintained by Qi, Jing still has an important role to play in our health. Chinese medicine teaches that Jing is stored in the Kidneys and is responsible for the cycles which allow us to grow, reproduce and develop. The way that we develop from babies to children is due to our Jing. It then helps us to move into puberty at adolescence and onto adulthood. Jing allows us to be fertile and for women to give birth. Later on, at the time of the female or male menopause, our Jing is in decline.

Jing and our reservoirs

The Jing also acts as a reservoir of energy and we draw on it during a crisis or periods of overwork. If we look after our health by eating well and balancing work, rest and exercise, then our reserves will remain fully stocked and we won't need to draw on them. They might even be topped up by some of the Qi which is formed from the food we eat and the air we breathe. If we overdo it, however, we will deplete our reserves of Jing. When the Jing gets depleted, this can result in us feeling drained of energy and easily becoming ill.

In this chapter we will be looking at:

1   how we can assess the strength of our Jing
2   how we deplete it
3   what we can do to conserve and replenish it
4   how we can improve its quality.

First, let's hear a little more about Jing itself.

Our Internal Battery

We can compare Jing to the battery of a car. Some people have a car and don't look after the battery. They drive it a lot at night, forget to switch the lights off when they stop or frequently use the radio, tape deck, cigarette lighter and other accessories. The battery quickly wears out. Others are more careful. They may use the car less frequently at night and always check that the lights are turned off before putting it away. A car that is well looked after will have a battery which lasts.

In the same way, our Jing is like our own internal battery. Some of us are careful and conserve our Jing while others use up their Jing by overdoing it. Unfortunately, it is easier to replace a car battery than our Jing.

Sarah's father is a good example of someone who has conserved his Jing:

My father is still a vigorous man at 86 years. His hair didn't turn gray until four years ago and he only started to feel he was getting a little old when he was 81. He's always led a healthy life and for meals he eats fresh food from our garden. Although he had a desk job he would always take a brisk walk for 40 minutes every day and at the weekends he would do sporting activities. I think I inherited some of his strong constitution but I'm not doing as well as he was at my age.

Keith now realizes that he drained his batteries in his teens:

I think my constitution was originally very strong. When I was young I rarely became ill and just naturally looked after myself by eating properly and getting enough sleep. Then when I was in my late teens I abused myself completely. I survived on very little sleep, was nearly an alcoholic, had too much sex and spent most of my time partying. I was lucky to get away with it. At the age of 20 I collapsed completely and I stayed in bed for almost a year. I can hardly remember that year. My mum nursed me. She described me as being in an 'emotional void'. I'm now 30 and have recovered, but I still have to be careful with myself. Sleep is important, as is eating regularly. I still think I need more sleep than other people so I make sure I get it. If I don't, I become very tired and get backache. It frustrates me a bit as I can't always do as much as I'd like, but I don't want to have a relapse.

Our Jing at Birth

Some of us are born with what seems to be an infinite amount of Jing while others start off with less. Most people's Jing is within the normal range. If we go back to the example of car engines, some cars have a large engine and others have a smaller one. Rolls Royce are renowned for making good quality engines. In the 1960s, however, a small car called the Mini was the most popular car in England. Although the Mini had a small engine it was still a very functional car. If it was well looked after, the Mini could last longer than many larger cars which hadn't been well cared for. Whether we have a large engine or a small engine when we are born, the main thing is that we conserve its power.

Using up our Jing

We can use up our Jing by living an irregular lifestyle or living to extremes. Anything that draws on our reserves of energy will exhaust our Jing. Eating a poor diet or eating irregularly, getting too little or irregular sleep, working too hard, playing too hard, long-term drug use, too much alcohol or even too much sex will all deplete us.

Keith described earlier how he drained himself by overdoing it in his teens. Here three more people tell us what they did.

James told me:

> I knew I always did more and worked harder than other people. At the time
> I thought I was very strong but in retrospect I think I was needy for a lot of
> things. I think others who didn't work as hard were more comfortable with
> themselves. In the end I wore myself out. I overworked, didn't get enough
> rest, had too much sex, ate irregularly and had a poor quality diet. I became
> diabetic and I knew I had to change.

Joan was also leading an irregular lifestyle.

> I used to have a very irregular lifestyle. I used to eat irregularly. I'd never have
> breakfast and then have my last meal at around 10 o'clock at night. I'd then
> go to bed at three in the morning.
>
> I thought it was normal. My whole family are night-owls and my mother
> still goes to bed really late. I had loads of illnesses, I was very tired, had
> hormonal problems, high blood-pressure and struggled with my weight the
> whole time. At that time I had no idea that changing my lifestyle would make
> a difference.

Finally, Teresa told me about her lifestyle:

> I think I've always had a slightly fragile constitution. In spite of this I'd always
> pushed myself and was often doing far too much. Finally I went on a course
> and kept going when it was too much for me. I became ill. I got overtired to

the point I couldn't sleep properly, then, when I couldn't sleep I'd be going to the toilet several times in the space of an hour. To keep going I took lots of caffeine and sugar and I was addicted to sleeping tablets for two years. I didn't want to listen to what my body was saying at first, but in the end I had to.

All of these people depleted their Jing. So what symptoms might we expect to see from this?

The Signs of a Depleted Constitution

The signs of the Jing becoming drained are the signs of aging. These include poor concentration and memory, inappropriate tiredness, premature graying hair or baldness (unless it is inherited), drying skin and wrinkles, brittle bones, tinnitus, dizziness, backache, constant colds, difficulty conceiving, an early menopause in women or impotence in men.

Those who are born with some deficiency of Jing might have a slight delay to the normal stages of their development. They may start walking or talking late and develop slowly as infants or the onset of puberty may be delayed. Another sign is that they might continually fall ill.

If we have 'normal' Jing but are depleting it, the first symptom we might experience is tiredness. Often people ignore this symptom. Our supply of Jing is finite. Many people who are born with a strong constitution don't realize this and think they have an infinite supply of energy, just as Keith did. Those who have a small 'engine' are often naturally more careful with themselves and in the end can outlast the people who started life with a larger battery. These are some of the ways we might use up our Jing:

- overwork
- not enough sleep
- too much sex
- too much exercise or overactivity
- severe long-term stress.

Although we can't restore the Jing we've used up, we can at least improve the quality of the Jing we still have.

Preserving our Jing

James, Joan and Teresa who talked to us earlier all changed their lifestyles and became healthier. Here they tell us what they did. James says:

> After I became diabetic I had to change my diet radically. I started eating regularly, and eating organic vegetables and other food. Other changes took longer. Now, 10 years later, I always make sure I get at least eight hours sleep at night and I do Qigong exercises every morning and sometimes in the evening. I now also work in a much less strenuous way although I still have a tendency to overwork at times. Before I was in a relationship where I wasn't getting my needs satisfied. I'm now in a loving relationship and that's made a big difference too.

Teresa tells us:

> The secret of looking after myself was definitely listening to my body. It took me a long time as I really didn't want to at first. The changes I've gradually made are in many ways to do with the quality of rest I get. I go to bed early, I enjoy going for walks more now and I take lots more holidays. I also try not to get overexcited about things and I meditate a lot. The main change I made to my diet was that I stopped taking caffeine and sugar. On the whole I really enjoy this lifestyle. Occasionally, when people are drinking coffee in the evening I know I'd like a cup, but I don't have one as I'd really suffer the consequences. I now sleep well and although I still get slightly tired sometimes I never get as tired as I was. A lot of the time my energy feels normal.

Joan can't believe the difference in herself:

> I've changed every aspect of my life. I've certainly changed my understanding of exercise. I do exercises which suit me. I do have quite a strong will and

before I would just push myself to the limit. If I know I'm tired I've learnt to recognize it and stop. I'll now eat at six or seven o'clock and I have three regular meals a day. The latest I'll go to bed is midnight. The changes happened gradually. I also had acupuncture treatment and the more I changed from treatment, the more I could make lifestyle changes and the more I changed my lifestyle, the better I became, so it was a positive cycle.

One of the best ways of preserving our Jing is to look after ourselves in the ways suggested in the previous chapters. Knowing when to work, rest and exercise and eating a sensible diet will contribute to our health and therefore help us to conserve our constitutional energy. The Chinese also suggest that we should balance our sexual activity.

Sexual Activity and our Jing

Some years ago I went to a seminar led by a well-known Chinese doctor who lives in New York. He diagnosed patients and suggested treatments skillfully. Many of the patients were very ill and each patient was given an individual diagnosis and treatment. There was only one statement that he made to almost everyone, it was, 'Don't have too much sex.'

In the West today the benefits of sex are widely publicized. It is understood that enjoying a satisfying sex life helps us to remain in close and fulfilling relationships. When we are ill or tired, however, we might consider making some temporary changes in order to regain our health.

Jing and orgasm

The Chinese say that sperm is a manifestation of Jing and that sexual activity takes a large amount of energy. Every time we have an orgasm we lose a small amount of Jing. This seems to apply slightly more to men, who lose sperm when they ejaculate. It does, however, also apply (to a lesser extent) to women. The Chinese doctor I mentioned earlier used to say, 'After a man has had an orgasm he needs to rest for a day. After a woman has had an orgasm she needs to rest for a few minutes!' This may be a slight exaggeration but nevertheless illustrates his point.

Sex and ill health

When we are well, it is healthy to have a sexual appetite. When we are ill, we need to cut down on our sexual activity to help us to regain our health. Some people naturally have less desire to have sex when they are ill or over-working and this is normal. Many feel that they should have more sexual appetite and deplete themselves trying to have a 'normal' amount of sex. Others try to please a partner who has a greater desire. A sympathetic partner will understand that the lack of desire is a sign of ill-health or a different constitution and not of rejection. This situation can, however, be a source of great friction for couples. This is especially true after the birth of a baby or during chronic illness and compromises need to be made.

'Too much' sex

Some people react differently. When they are tense and overworked they have a heightened desire for sex. They may find this build up of tension can be released through orgasm. In this situation they may be engaging in too much sexual activity which may be temporarily satisfying but in the long-term may drain them. This can produce a vicious circle which is hard to break. They initially get tense because they are stressed and tired but ultimately become more tired and stressed due to too much sex. When this is the case the person needs to deal with the underlying causes of the tension.

The benefits of sex

The benefits of sex are also important. Sexual closeness is of course a way to create intimacy within a relationship and this will lead to better health. Sex can also be an important way to release tension, as long as it is not used in this way habitually. When people have tight muscles, orgasm can relax them and may free up blocked energy and even cure pain. The frustration which can build up through a lack of sexual activity can be just as damaging to our health as too much sex.

Age and sex

As well as giving us guidelines about sexual activity when we are unwell, Chinese books discuss what constitutes a normal sex life at different stages in our lives. All the ancient Chinese doctors had different opinions however! In general it is normal for younger people to enjoy a more active sex life and for this to steadily decline as a person gets older. As a rule of thumb, a maximum frequency of ejaculation for a man in good health at the age of 20 would be twice a day, at 30 once a day, at 40 every three days, at 50 every five days, at 60 every 10 days and at 70 every 30 days. This should be doubled if the person is unwell or tired.[1]

Sex and the seasons

It is best that our sexual activity also changes with the seasons. It is normal to enjoy more sex during the summer when it is hotter and have less sexual activity in the colder months.

Our Jing in Pregnancy and Childbirth

Just as men use up Jing when they ejaculate, pregnancy depletes a woman's Jing. A baby receives nourishment from its mother's Jing whilst it is in the womb. If the mother doesn't rest, eat well and generally care for herself, she may start to deplete her reserves. Chinese mothers also stress the importance of resting after giving birth (*see page 109*).

Nourishing ourselves during pregnancy

Mothers who don't rest during pregnancy or who have many pregnancies close together may find they develop signs of Jing deficiency. Symptoms such as aging skin, graying hair, breaking nails and extreme tiredness may result. On the other hand a mother who nourishes herself properly may end up healthier than before she became pregnant.

Jing and miscarriages

Chinese medicine teaches that miscarriage is even more depleting for a woman than pregnancy itself. This is because the natural cycle of pregnancy has been cut short. A woman often needs to go through a huge psychological as well as physical adjustment following a miscarriage. Often her instinct is to become pregnant again as soon as possible to make up for the loss. A healthier option for her is to rest and recover from the grief.

If she becomes pregnant again before she is ready, the baby may have weaker Jing or the mother may become more depleted and tired. Allowing at least six months or even a year to recover from a miscarriage will enable a mother to fully regain her energy and overcome the loss.

Motherhood is a time when women can blossom and improve their health – or a time when they can lose it. Parenthood can also be an important turning point for both mother and father as they care for and nourish their newborn infant.

Four Important Stages in our Lives

Besides pregnancy and childbirth there are three other major times in our lives when our health can substantially change. The major times are:

1 puberty
2 leaving home
3 pregnancy and childbirth
4 menopause.

These are times when transformations are occurring either physically or psychologically. If we care for our health during these periods we can end up feeling rejuvenated and healthier. If, on the other hand, we ignore our health needs, we may become less well.

Some people, for example, blossom when they come into puberty. Others find that it is a difficult time from which they never truly recover. A lot of women feel unwell throughout their menopause while for others it is the beginning of the healthiest time of their lives.

These four phases are important, but a healthy lifestyle is best if it becomes a lifelong habit. Below are suggestions which we can all observe. They will enable us to safeguard our Jing at every stage of our lives.

Living within the Confines of our Jing

Here are four guidelines which will help us to conserve our constitutional energy and not go beyond our limits.

1 Only do things which we know are within our capacity and listen to our body's needs.
2 Avoid comparing our capacity to someone else's.
3 Even if we have lots of energy and Jing, preserve it by paying attention to our health now.
4 If we have depleted our Jing it is advisable to get Chinese medical help to restore ourselves.

Listen to your body's needs

Many people think it's normal to overwork. Often they override their exhaustion and keep active instead of resting. Once we are in the habit of overworking it becomes more difficult to stop. There is often conflict between the needs of family and work. Theresa told me, 'Listening to my body was the key to my getting better.' She also said, 'It took me a long time to take notice and I didn't want to at first.' This is true for many of us and often we don't think we can slow down, yet we can find time to do what we need to and at least make some healthy adjustments to our lifestyles.

Never compare your capacity to someone else's

If we have the engine of a Mini, or we have a larger car with batteries which are run down, then it's best to accept the situation and work within our limits. If we look at other people who we think have Rolls Royce engines and expect to be like them, we will always find ourselves wanting. If we compare ourselves only to ourselves, we will know that what we achieve is within our own capacity. This will enable us to feel proud of what we have done and able to get the best from our lives.

Pay attention to your health now

Our health is our insurance policy. Many people take their good health for granted. If a crisis arises out of the blue, we can deal with it better if our battery is fully charged beforehand. If our batteries are already going flat we may be left completely depleted afterwards. When we are depleted, we are more vulnerable to illness. Even if we think we have loads of energy and vitality, a healthy lifestyle will keep it that way rather than depleting us when we most need it.

Restore your strength with Chinese medicine

Acupuncture can tonify our energy and there are many Chinese herbal medicines that can strengthen us too. Unfortunately, there are very few tonics left in Western medicine. Western drugs tend to take away symptoms but won't restore our energy. Chinese medicine understands the need for tonics. Joan found that when she had acupuncture treatment, as well as changing her lifestyle, the treatment gave her the strength to carry out the changes needed to restore her health. When we are really depleted and unwell, a change in our lifestyle may be difficult to undertake and it may not be enough to get us back to health.

Strengthening the Quality of our Jing

As well as ensuring that we eat healthily and have enough work, rest and exercise, the Chinese suggest that we can strengthen the quality of our Jing with Chinese exercises such as Qigong or Tai Ji Quan.

We can improve the quality of our Jing by activating an area one or two inches below the umbilicus called the 'Tan Tien'. The Chinese call the Tan Tien 'the seat of the Jing'. By practicing Chinese exercises we can improve our vitality and well-being and become more relaxed.

Activating the Tan Tien

When the Tan Tien is activated, a vibration may be felt in the area and it can become warmer. There are three main ways to activate the Tan Tien:

1 breathing into our Tan Tien
2 adjusting our posture
3 focusing our attention on the Tan Tien.

We'll look at each of these in turn.

Breathing into Tan Tien

Natural deep breathing into the lower abdomen relaxes us and this in turn builds our energy. To breathe into the lower abdomen, breathe in through the nose and at the same time allow the lower abdomen and sides to expand. Then breathe out and allow the abdomen to relax. Breathing in this way is natural and easy. At the same time it will move the area of the lower abdomen and activate the Tan Tien.[2]

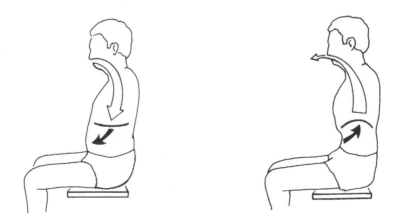

Figures 11a, 11b: Breathing in and out from the Tan Tien.

Adjusting our posture

Adjusting our posture ensures that our center of gravity naturally falls to the Tan Tien and will also aid its activation. For the basic standing position, stand with the feet facing forward and shoulder width apart. Bend the knees slightly so that they are unlocked. Relax the hips and lower abdomen and allow the weight to travel down to the arches of the feet. Allow the pelvis to curl slightly forward so that the lower back is straight. Relax the shoulders and neck and let the arms hang loosely at the sides. Keep the head upright and look straight ahead.[3]

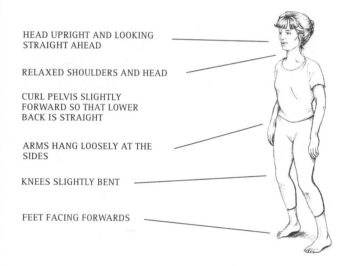

HEAD UPRIGHT AND LOOKING
STRAIGHT AHEAD

RELAXED SHOULDERS AND HEAD

CURL PELVIS SLIGHTLY
FORWARD SO THAT LOWER
BACK IS STRAIGHT

ARMS HANG LOOSELY AT THE
SIDES

KNEES SLIGHTLY BENT

FEET FACING FORWARDS

Figure 12: Adjusting posture during Qigong exercises.

Focusing our attention

Focusing our attention on the Tan Tien is also a simple yet effective way to strengthen it. Below is a simple exercise which will help us to place our attention on the Tan Tien.

A Qigong Exercise for the Tan Tien

As well as focusing our attention on the Tan Tien, this exercise will aid our concentration, strengthen our Qi field to help ward off infections and enable us to develop the ability to direct our Qi inside and outside our body.

1   Stand in the basic standing posture pictured above.
2   Imagine that your Qi is extending outwards from your Tan Tien, in all directions. You might imagine your Qi as a colored light, or just get a 'sense' of the energy.
3   As the Qi expands feel your arms and hands slowly moving outwards. Expand your arms wider and wider until you are reaching out to the universe.
4   Feel your energy extended to the universe and at the same time notice you can remain centered in your lower abdomen.

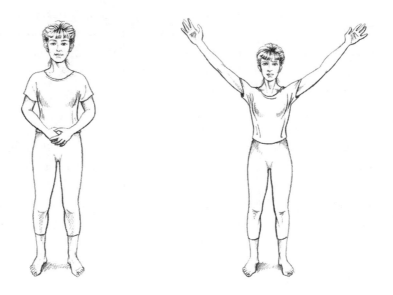

Figures 13a, 13b: A Qigong Exercise for the Tan Tien

5 Now allow the Qi from the universe to contract. As it comes in allow it to move your arms inwards until the Qi is in your Tan Tien and is getting smaller and smaller but never disappearing.

6 Repeat for 5 to 10 minutes continuing to allow the Qi to expand and contract.

Qigong and Jing

Finding a Qigong teacher

Basic Qi exercises are simple and safe to do. If we wish to progress in the practice of Qigong or Tai Ji Quan, however, it is always best to do so under the guidance of an experienced teacher. By having a teacher we can develop strong internal stability and strength whatever size engine we have, which in turn will improve our health. As our Jing is strengthened in its quality, we will have more vitality, our energy will become better focused and our mind clearer.[4]

The best way to find a teacher is via other people's recommendations. You may wish to talk to the pupils and find out about the benefits they reap from their practice. Before joining a class you might want to talk to the teacher to find out more about the kind of Qigong practice she or he teaches. Some addresses of teachers are listed at the end of this book.

Longevity through Qi exercises

Chinese books are full of stories of people who restored their Jing with Chinese exercises. One story is of a Chinese man who came from a poor family. He had to sell vegetables at the local fair from a young age and he carried them on a pole which rested on his shoulders. By the time he was 12 he had developed a hunched back and was nicknamed 'the hunchbacked vegetable boy'. He later learned Chinese boxing – a martial art where concentration on the Tan Tien is practiced. He eventually straightened his back. He was still strong and robust at 100 and taught other children Chinese boxing throughout his life.[5]

Another story is of a doctor who became weakened when he developed tuberculosis at the age of 48. He practiced Qigong under a famous teacher. By learning Qigong his lung trouble cleared without any treatment and he subsequently became a practitioner of Chinese medicine and worked until he was nearly 100 years old.[6]

Checking the Strength of our Jing

Chinese medicine also gives us guidelines which help us to assess the overall strength of our constitution. The three main ways to assess this are:

1   the length of our earlobes
2   the strength of our jaw line
3   our overall stamina.

Constitution and the Ears

Ancient Chinese texts talk about the size of the ears and the length of the earlobes as a guide to the strength of the Jing. The ears should be well placed – that is not too high on the head. They should also be a good size in relation to the person's build. The earlobes should also be long.

If we look at Oriental pictures of the Buddha, he is often depicted as having huge earlobes – perhaps signifying the extraordinary strength of his essence. While long and full lobes are said to indicate a strong constitution, small thin earlobes are said to indicate a less strong one.

The Strength of the Jaw Line

A large head on a strong broad jaw line is also indicative of a healthy constitution. According to Chinese facial diagnosis, the jaw and lower part of the face relate to the later years of a person's life. This can be used as an approximate guide to how we will fare in old age. A strong jaw indicates that we will have a long life, remain healthy into old age and easily recover from illness. A weak jaw means we might be less healthy.

151

Figure 14: Buddha with long earlobes.

We can observe the ear and the jaw line to roughly assess how we will deal with illnesses later on in life. If both are of good size and shape we should fare well. If not, we might start to prepare ourselves now and build up our Jing in order to have a healthy future.

Our Physique and Stamina

One other useful way of assessing the strength of our Jing is to consider our overall stamina. If we are very robust, have a naturally strong physique and can easily work hard and recover our energy quickly, this may indicate that we have strong Jing.

Those people who have these 'high quality' engines may sometimes fail to understand the fragility of the rest of the population who have weaker or even normal constitutional energy. They may wonder why we can't just 'pull ourselves together and get on with life' when we are under stress or are ill. A person with strong Jing will easily recover from illness. If we have an abundant supply of Jing, we should still be careful. Our Jing is finite and if we overdo it, we too can end up exhausting ourselves. Those frailer people who are looking after their health now might fare better in the future.

For a questionnaire about our constitution see 'How Strong is My Constitution?' on page 218.

Summary

1   We use up our Jing by living an excessive or irregular life in relation to diet, work, rest, exercise and sexual activity. We can preserve our Jing by living healthily.
2   Premature signs of aging, excessive depletion or continual ill health indicate that we are using up our Jing.
3   If we have a frail constitution from birth we may develop more slowly than others and easily succumb to illness even as a child.
4   Four guidelines which will help us to conserve our constitutional energy are:
    • only do things that we know are within our capacity
    • compare ourselves only to ourselves
    • pay attention to our health now
    • get Chinese medical help if we have depleted our Jing.
5   We can improve the quality of our Jing by practicing Qi exercises and strengthening our Tan Tien in the lower abdomen.
6   Our ears, jaw line and stamina are all rough indicators of the strength of our constitution.

Staying Healthy and
Preventing Disease

This chapter will provide a reference for many common ailments. It lists the common Chinese diagnoses for these conditions and some lifestyle adjustments to improve or prevent them. These suggestions are not meant as a substitute for medical help, nor are they a substitute for Chinese treatments such as acupuncture, Chinese herbs or Chinese massage (Tuina).

Chinese treatments can be extremely effective for many of these complaints. Once treated, patients can then prevent recurrence of the problem by making appropriate lifestyle changes. I will be considering these conditions:

anxiety and panic attacks   hypertension
asthma   indigestion and heartburn
back pain   insomnia
colds and flu   joint problems
constipation   menopausal hot flushes
depression   period pains
diabetes   post-viral syndromes
diarrhea   premenstrual syndrome
headaches   skin conditions.

At the end of each section I have written which Chinese medicines can be used to help each complaint. I have abbreviated as follows:

A – Acupuncture
CH – Chinese herbs
TM – Tuina massage

Anxiety and Panic Attacks

Chinese medicine diagnosis

According to Chinese medicine, anxiety or panic attacks are most often caused by:

Blood deficiency
The Blood of the Heart houses our Spirit. If the Blood is deficient the Spirit becomes unsettled, causing anxiety or panics.

Yin deficiency
Yin energy cools us and calms us down, whilst Yang energy warms us and gets us moving. If the cooling and calming Yin energy is deficient it will cause a person to become restless, causing anxiety or panics.

Lifestyle changes which may prevent or improve anxiety and panic attacks

Diet
Vegetarians may not be eating enough 'Blood' nourishing food. This can cause Blood deficiency which can lead to anxiety and panic attacks. Those vegetarians who have no ethical reasons for not eating meat are advised to start eating a small amount of meat, poultry or fish. This could produce tremendous benefits for their emotional health. For more on eating meat see page 25. Do not expect an immediate change as it may take a few weeks or months for the Blood to build up in the system.

For those who are vegetarian and who prefer not to eat meat see page 27 for Hints for Vegetarians. Eating a nourishing diet, rich in fresh vegetables and grains is essential for anyone who has panic attacks or anxiety, whether they are vegetarian or not. We also need to make sure that we:

1 don't skip meals
2 eat three meals regularly every day
3 eat in a relaxed environment.

Caffeine

Excessive amounts of caffeine from drinking tea, coffee, hot chocolate and colas can also cause some people to become overanxious. To discover whether these are having a negative effect on our health we can try cutting them out for two or three weeks. At the end of this time we can assess whether there is a difference and we may decide to continue to exclude them from our diet.

Relaxation and rest

Sometimes if we are living an overactive lifestyle or have a highly stressful job this can culminate in anxiety and panics. We can put aside time for relaxation before going to bed and take at least eight hours rest in bed, even if we have difficulty sleeping. It is also beneficial to ensure that we take sufficient breaks for lunch and have a rest after lunch. Our bodies can create better quality Blood if we relax and rest.

Bleeding

Any bleeding can cause Blood deficiency. Many women who use a coil find that they bleed profusely during their periods. This can cause the Blood to become deficient. If this is the case, a change of contraception may be necessary. Heavy periods or bleeding during childbirth can also cause Blood deficiency and can be a common cause of post-natal anxiety or depression. In this case we can eat more Blood nourishing foods (*see page 25*). If we have lost a lot of Blood or are continuing to have heavy periods it may be necessary to have Chinese medicine treatments such as Chinese herbs or acupuncture.

Qigong and Tai Ji Quan

Qigong and Tai Ji Quan are relaxing exercises that can have a profound effect on those who feel anxious. By carrying out the gentle exercises and strengthening the Tan Tien in the lower abdomen we can learn to become calmer and more settled (*see Activating the Tan Tien on page 147*).

Chinese medicine treatment
A, CH and TM.

Asthma

Chinese medicine diagnosis

The Chinese describe asthma as 'xiao' which means wheezing combined with 'chuan' which means breathlessness. Asthma can be caused either by:

Qi deficiency
Deficient Lung Qi is most common, but deficient Spleen or Kidney Qi may also be a cause of asthma.

Phlegm
Phlegm can be caught in the chest causing wheezing.

Wind-Cold or Wind-Heat
Mild asthma can be exacerbated into a full-blown asthma attack by catching a cold or flu. The Chinese refer to colds and flu as Wind-Cold or Wind-Heat (*see page 119*). The Wind-Cold or Wind-Heat must be cleared from the body for a person to recover and bring the asthma back to manageable levels. If it is not cleared, the asthma will intensify and this will further weaken the already fragile Lungs (*see also Colds and Flu on page 162*).

Lifestyle changes which may prevent or improve asthma

Diet
Many people with asthma have Phlegm caught in the chest but are not aware of it. Asthma symptoms can often be reduced by cutting out Phlegm and Damp-forming foods especially dairy products (*see page 22*) which create a lot of mucus. Oranges are also known to exacerbate phlegm on the chest. We can take care not to eat too much cold food or sweet foods such as iced fizzy drinks and chocolates as these can weaken our Spleen Qi, which in turn depletes the energy in our Lungs.

Some asthma is triggered by an intolerance to certain foods or food additives. Those who get an asthma attack after eating one or more foods can do the following:

1   try removing one or more of the suspect foods from the diet completely for a few weeks
2   notice if the asthma recedes during this time
3   if the asthma recedes, cut out the food(s) for a longer period and watch to see if the asthma abates still more.

Food allergies can occur by eating an excessive amount of one type of food over long periods or if at an early age we were given food that our digestive system was not mature enough to digest. If we crave one particular food this may be a sign that we are allergic to it. We may need to give up the very food we most enjoy in order to overcome the symptoms of intolerance.

We also need to eat a nourishing diet which is rich in fresh vegetables and grains (*see page 18*). This will strengthen our Qi and help to prevent asthma attacks.

Protection from the environment

Most asthma sufferers know that catching a cold can intensify and trigger asthma which is otherwise latent. Wearing a scarf in windy weather, wearing a vest in the cold, covering the hands and feet and never leaving the chest exposed to the environment are all essential to anyone who has asthma. For more about protecting ourselves from the environment read Chapter 5, pages 111–134.

Over–activity and rest

Inhalers allow many people with asthma to lead a normal life. However, an asthma attack is also a 'signal' that there is an underlying cause which needs to be dealt with. An inhaler temporarily alleviates the symptom but does not address the cause. Sometimes the relief gained from using an inhaler allows us to do more than is within our true capacity. This can ultimately deplete our Qi. Those who have asthma are advised to guard against doing too much and take regular rests.

Emotions

Asthma can be aggravated by stress or emotional problems. If this is the case, we can take notice of the specific trigger. It can often be unexpressed frustration or anger but may also be grief, anxiety or other emotions. Once we know what provokes an attack we can examine our lifestyle and decide how best we can deal with the stress. We can also strive to avoid getting into situations which trigger the emotions. Read Chapter 3 of this book to find other ways of dealing with emotional strains.

Qigong and other exercises

Mild exercise can often help people with asthma. For those who get no exercise at all, it is a good idea to start learning Tai Ji Quan or Qigong as this can strengthen the chest. Strong exercise is not recommended, especially if the lungs are weak, as this may put too much strain on them.

Good posture

Asthma is sometimes caused or worsened by poor posture, especially during childhood. Children can be stooping over books, sitting on wrongly adjusted seats or watching television for long periods. In these situations they may not breathe properly because they are putting undue pressure on their chests. Adjusting the posture can be beneficial in these cases. Encouraging more breaks for activity can also help to encourage proper breathing.

Pollutants

Pollutants in the air will exacerbate an asthma attack. Living in an urban area can be especially stressful on the lungs but country areas can also be polluted, particularly during crop spraying. Household paint and other products which contain strong chemicals can also give off noxious fumes which can trigger attacks and even household cleaners can cause problems. House dust mites are also said to be one of the most common causes of asthma attacks. It is important to keep the environment of anyone with asthma free of any of these particles and pollutants.

Smoking

Anyone who has asthma is advised to stop smoking. Smoking weakens the Lung Qi and causes further difficulty breathing.

Chinese medicine treatment
A and CH.

Back Pain

Chinese medicine diagnosis

Backaches are one of the commonest reasons given for absenteeism from work in the Western world. Chinese medicine teaches that there are many causes. The main reasons for backache are:

Deficient Kidney Qi
The Kidneys are situated in our lower back. If they are functioning sluggishly then we will have a dull ache in this area.

Qi and Blood 'Stagnation' in the lower back
Sometimes back problems are caused by either mental or physical overstrain. We develop tense muscles in the lower back as we try to cope with our problems or overstrain ourselves physically. This prevents our Qi and Blood from moving, which in turn causes pain. The pain can develop slowly or the back can suddenly become 'sprained' and we can find ourselves unable to move. Anyone who has suffered from this acute sprain will testify to its extreme pain.

Wind, Cold and/or Damp in the lower back
This can cause acute or chronic back pain.

Physical trauma
A sports injury or an accident is a common cause of back problems.

Wind and Cold in the neck
This can be a cause of acute neck pain.

Lifestyle changes which may prevent or improve back pain

Posture
Bad posture can either cause or exacerbate a back problem. When lifting we should bend the knees rather than the back. Lifting heavy weights can also

strain the back and using labor saving devices such as shopping baskets with wheels can save us from developing back problems later on.

People who have back problems are advised to use chairs which support the back and try not to sit in a slumped position. Sitting incorrectly for long periods of time will exacerbate a back problem.

The back can also become weak after prolonged periods of standing. In this case it is best to adjust our lifestyle so that we sit down more frequently. People who are in jobs which entail long periods of standing, such as nurses, teachers or shop assistants, may find it necessary to transfer to alternative, less strenuous work. Those who think that posture has contributed to their back problems may find it helpful to see someone who specializes in the Alexander technique.

Protection from the environment

Wind, Cold and Damp commonly affect the lower back. For example, when we are gardening we may build up a sweat and remove clothes. This can leave the back exposed. As we cool down afterwards, the Wind, Cold and Damp can enter the back through the open pores. Cold causes the tissues to contract, creating acute pain and the Wind and Damp also contribute. Similar conditions affect people working on building sites, people sunning themselves on a hot day which then turns cool or after exercising and working up a sweat. We can make sure to cover up the lower back to protect it from Wind, Cold and Damp. If necessary place a hot pad or hot bottle on the back if it starts to become painful following such events.

Sleeping in a draught can also cause neck pain. Never sleep under a fan or next to an open window as Wind and Cold can penetrate the neck.

Rest and relaxation

Overactivity, especially when carried out under stress, can also cause backache. The stress will cause the muscles to tighten up and the strenuous activity will weaken them. We need to make sure that we get enough rest, especially if we are working hard physically. Sleeping in a good posture is also essential. Some people with back problems find lying on their back is the best sleeping position.

Emotions

The spine is the central pillar which holds us erect and our emotions are often reflected there. If the cause of a back problem is emotional then we may find that dealing with our emotions can help to clear the physical problem. For example, if we are depressed, we can feel slumped inside and this can depress the spine. If we are angry, we can tighten up and tense the muscles in the back. The Chinese associate fear with the Kidneys and the function of this organ is associated with the spine. When we are afraid we can feel 'spineless' and have a weakened back. We can also pull away from things which make us afraid and this can put a strain on our back (*see page 52 for more on our emotions*).

Exercise

Gentle exercise such as Tai Ji Quan or Qigong can help to relax a tight back or strengthen a weak one. It is essential to do the exercises in the correct posture with the back relaxed and straight pelvis tilted towards the ground (*see page 148*). Gentle stretching exercises can also be beneficial.

Strenuous exercise such as lifting weights, vigorous jogging or energetic racket games can aggravate a back problem and anyone with a weak back should avoid these exercises.

Chinese medicine treatment
A and TM.

Other treatments

Although not a part of Chinese medicine, chiropractic, osteopathy and craniosacral therapy need to be mentioned here as they can also be beneficial for many back problems. Alexander technique (mentioned above) can also be helpful.

Colds and Flu

Chinese medicine diagnosis

If we keep ourselves healthy we will have strong 'Wei' Qi or defensive Qi. This defensive Qi lies just between the skin and muscles and protects us from the invasion of 'Wind' from the environment. Colds and flu are either caused by Wind-Cold or Wind-Heat:

Wind-Cold
This will give us symptoms such as a stuffy nose with clear white mucus, an itchy throat, sneezing, coughing, a slight headache at the base of the skull, a desire to keep warm and/or slightly achy joints.

Wind-Heat
This is often more severe and similar to influenza. We might feel hot and feverish as well as sweaty and thirsty and have swollen tonsils or a sore throat. We might also have a stuffy or runny nose with yellow mucus, fairly severe joint pains as well as a desire to keep warm.

For more on the effects of Wind see Chapter 5 on Protection from the Environment. The best 'treatment' for a cold or flu is prevention.

Lifestyle changes which may prevent or improve colds and flu

Protection from climatic factors
We are vulnerable to catching colds and flu when there is a change in temperature. To prevent them, we can make sure that we wear appropriate clothes when going in and out of buildings, when we return to a cold climate from sunny holidays or when the weather changes unseasonably.

We are also more vulnerable when we are in windy weather conditions. Windy weather to the Chinese can be anything from the actual wind, to draughts, the air blowing from a fan or air conditioning. The neck area is very vulnerable to the effects of Wind. When we are in these environments we need to cover the neck.

Stress
If we are under stress our defensive Qi (and therefore the immune system) is weakened and we become vulnerable to catching colds and flu (*see Chapter 3, page 57*). During these stressful times in our lives we are often most neglectful of our health (*see Chapter 3, page 60 for a list of common stressors in our lives*). These are times that we really need to be particularly vigilant and make sure we eat properly and get enough rest and sleep to guard against illness.

Overwork and rest

When we overwork our Qi becomes depleted. This causes our defensive Qi to weaken and makes us more vulnerable to catching colds. A cold can swiftly affect everyone in our working environment, especially if the people in it are overworked and under stress.

If we are ill with a cold it is best to drop everything and rest. This will often stop the cold from developing. If the cold does develop it is advisable to take time off work to convalesce. If we ensure that we have fully recovered our health before returning to work, we will be less vulnerable to more infections. It will also save our work colleagues from also becoming infected and prevent an epidemic from occurring all around the building.

Clearing a cold

Wind-Cold needs to be dealt with in a different way from Wind-Heat. The symptoms of each are listed above in 'Chinese medicine diagnosis'.

Wind-Cold

A person who has a Wind-Cold needs to sweat in order to eliminate the Wind from the body through the pores. A ginger tea will encourage us to sweat. To make a ginger tea:

1 place 3–5 slices of ginger in a cup
2 pour boiling water in it
3 leave it to brew for about 5 minutes
4 add 1 teaspoonful of honey.

Alternatively, an old fashioned 'hot toddy' will have the same effect. To make a hot toddy mix together a capful of whisky with a teaspoonful of honey in boiling water.

After taking these remedies it is important to keep warm while the pores are opened to let out the cold. A herbal remedy to do this is called 'Expel Wind-Cold' obtainable in England from East-West Herbs (*see Useful Addresses, page 241*).

Wind-Heat

A peppermint tea will help to clear Wind-Heat:

1   place 1 peppermint teabag in boiling water
2   add 1 teaspoonful of honey
3   leave for five minutes.

In order to clear Wind-Heat, there are two herbal remedies which can be effective. One is called 'Yin Qiao San' and the other is called 'Expel Wind-Heat' (*see Useful Addresses, page 241*). These will clear the first sign of a sore throat before it turns into flu.

Although the best 'treatment' for a cold is prevention, once we have a cold it is important to clear it from the system. We can keep the Chinese herbal remedies suggested above in our medicine cabinet and take them at the first sign of a cold. Colds which are not cleared can travel deeper into the body and weaken the lungs. Long term use of antibiotics will also weaken our immune system and lead to weak lungs.

Chinese medicine treatment
A and CH.

Chinese herbal medicine can treat colds and flu and can be used to both strengthen the defensive Qi to prevent colds as well as for clearing colds from the body. The herbal prescriptions described are only two of many that can be prescribed for colds and flu. Acupuncture can also be used in a similar way and can treat both colds and flu and help strengthen the body to prevent infections.

Constipation

Chinese medicine diagnosis

It is normal to open our bowels regularly every day. If we open them less frequently or have difficulty expelling the stool then we are constipated. Some people can only open their bowels with the help of laxatives. If this is the case, it is better to find natural ways to open our bowels and become less dependent on pills.

Constipation has many causes – these are some of the main ones:

Deficient Spleen Qi

The Spleen Qi is responsible for transforming and moving food and drink throughout the body. If this transforming and moving function is weak then the bowel will be sluggish.

Blood deficiency

One of the functions of Blood is to moisturize our system. If we are Blood deficient then the bowels can lack moisture, creating constipation.

Qi Stagnation in the lower abdomen

The Liver Qi keeps our energy flowing smoothly. If the Liver is not functioning well, the Qi may stagnate, causing constipation.

Heat in the lower abdomen

This dries up the stool, causing constipation.

Cold in the lower abdomen

Heat creates movement and Cold slows movement down. If the lower abdomen is too cold this can cause the normal movement to slow down.

Lifestyle changes which may prevent or improve constipation

Diet

Diet is especially important in the treatment of constipation. It is best if our diet is well-proportioned and full of fresh vegetables, whole grains, beans and fruit. This diet will provide fiber which is essential for normal bowel movements. Those who have a tendency to constipation need to beware of eating processed food or 'fast foods' which contain very little fiber and nourishment.

Any extremes of diet can also be the cause of constipation. We can look at our diet and notice if we are eating too much Cooling or Heating food or are eating too much of one taste in our diet. An excess of Heating foods can dry up the stools whilst too much Cooling food can slow them down. Excess Phlegm and Damp-forming food can slow down the Spleen's transforming and transporting process causing constipation (*see Chapter 2 for more about diet*).

Emotional stress

Unexpressed emotions or any emotional 'holding on' over long periods of time may start to reflect physically in our bowels and cause us to become constipated. This may be especially true if we are harboring anger, resentment or frustration, but can also be unexpressed grief, sadness or other emotions. Looking at our lives and discovering whether there are unresolved emotions may free us up mentally. This may then reflect on us physically with easier bowel movements.

Exercise

A static lifestyle can cause constipation. Regular light exercise is important for anyone who is constipated as it encourages bowel movements.

Overwork

The Spleen is responsible for all transformation and movement in the body. If we overwork we can weaken the Spleen so that it can no longer move and transform. This can cause the bowels to become sluggish. If this is the case, it is important to get enough rest and to eat in the right conditions.

Regularity

The best time to open the bowels is in the morning and we can try to develop this at a regular time each day. Some people find it difficult to open their bowels in strange environments or away from home. If we develop the morning as a regular time, we will normally be opening the bowels before leaving home and this may help to overcome such problems.

Chinese medicine treatment
CH, A and TM.

Depression

Chinese medicine diagnosis

Chinese medicine teaches that there are many causes of depression. These are the most common causes:

'Stagnation' of the Liver Qi

The Liver is responsible for keeping our Qi flowing smoothly throughout our system. If we become frustrated, angry, resentful or hold in our emotions this may cause them to implode and our Qi to stop flowing freely, thus causing depression.

Qi deficiency

Feeling depressed can also be caused by the Qi becoming deficient. This is especially true of the Heart Qi or the Lung Qi. If the Heart Qi is weak we may feel dull and lacking in joy and vitality. If the Lung Qi is weak we may lack energy and become depleted and depressed as we are unable to take revitalizing fresh air into the lungs.

Dampness

Dampness can prevent the Qi from flowing easily which in turn causes depression.

Lifestyle changes which may prevent or improve depression

Emotions

Depression can vary from low grade depression to a depression which is so debilitating that it is impossible to move or function without help. It can initially be brought on by outside circumstances such as a relationship break up, the death of a loved one, difficulties at work or financial worries.

Dealing with the grief, worry or anxiety is an essential part of the healing process. In this case our friends and family are often our greatest support and can help us by listening and allowing us to express our problems and worries (*see Talking Therapy, page 68*).

Sometimes it is hard to say what has caused depression, but once in this state, it is hard to lift out of it. A common cause is unexpressed anger. If this implosion of emotions is recognized and the feelings articulated, it will often help to clear it. There are some suggestions on pages 68–75 which will help us to do this.

Writing a daily journal or getting more perspective on our problems can also help us to deal with our feelings of depression. In some circumstances it may be best to get the help of a trained counselor or therapist. Acupuncture or Chinese herbs can also be tremendously helpful.

Exercise and movement

Depression which is caused by Stagnation of the Liver Qi will often lift if we get moving. Any exercise including some brisk walking, swimming, playing a racket game, Tai Qi Quan or Qigong will be helpful. Someone who is feeling low does not always find it easy to get up and start exercising. Once they start moving, however, and the energy starts flowing again, they will feel better. A friend or partner can be a useful resource and can persuade us to become more active.

Diet

A regular diet rich in fresh vegetables, grains and beans will help us to become healthier and to build our Qi to prevent depression. Phlegm and Damp-forming foods can especially block up the system and cause a person to feel heavy and lethargic. We can try cutting these from our diet for a month to find out if they are exacerbating our emotional state.

Alcohol

Drinking alcohol can relax a person. Many people say it frees them up and makes them feel less depressed. Long term, however, alcohol can have a depressing effect. Stagnation of the Liver energy is often a cause of depression and alcohol can increase this stagnation.

Climate

Some people are affected by damp weather and find that they become more depressed when the weather is damp and gloomy for long periods. People who live in Damp houses can also become depressed (*see page 124*). A dehumidifier in the house will help to clear the dampness from the environment. This may in turn brighten the spirits.

Chinese medicine treatment

A, CH and TM.

Diabetes

Chinese and Western medicine diagnosis

A healthy lifestyle is an essential ingredient in both the prevention and management of diabetes. Amazingly, Chinese medical books first described the treatment of diabetes which was called 'Wasting and Thirsting Disease', 2,000 years ago.

There are two types of diabetes described in Western medicine. One is known as 'Type 1' diabetes and the other as 'Type 2' diabetes. Those who have the Type 1 diabetes are often diagnosed following an excessive weight loss, extreme thirst, excessive appetite and frequent urination. This is commonly found in young people although it can affect people of any age group. People with this type of diabetes will treat themselves by injecting insulin. Chinese medicine teaches that these extreme symptoms indicate that the person is overheating. Hence the name 'wasting and thirsting' disease.

Type 2 diabetes is usually slower in onset and often affects older people who are overweight. Those with this type of diabetes may not show any symptoms although some people complain of vague tiredness and needing to urinate at night. Most often it is found following a urine test. The treatment for this type of diabetes is usually dietary or prescribed tablets. Sometimes people with Type 2 diabetes will be treated with insulin injections. More young people are now getting Type 2 diabetes as the incidence of obesity increases.

Lifestyle changes which may prevent or improve diabetes

Prevention and management
The lifestyle changes required in the management of diabetes are much the same as those needed to prevent it. Chinese medicine describes the main causes of diabetes as:

1   an irregular lifestyle
2   poor diet
3   overwork
4   stress
5   too much sex.

By following the guidelines below, a person who has Type 1 diabetes can ensure that they remain healthy with as few side-effects as possible. Although the person is unlikely to come off their insulin completely, they will usually have far better sugar control. They may also be able to reduce their intake of insulin.

People who have Type 2 diabetes will also usually find that they have better control over their diabetes. Often they can lose weight and will have consistently lower readings when testing their blood sugar. Some common side effects of diabetes include kidney disease, eye problems and nerve damage. Lifestyle changes will reduce these risks.

Diet

A healthy diet is an essential part of the regime of any diabetic. It is essential for insulin dependent diabetics to carefully balance their diet with their insulin requirements to avoid swings in their blood sugar. The diet described in Chapter 2 on page 14 is very similar in proportion and content to the diet now recommended to diabetics. Eating a diet high in carbohydrates and low in fat has been found to help the sugar control of people who have diabetes and also cut down side effects. It can also enable a non-insulin dependent diabetic to lose weight if necessary. A useful book is *The Diabetic Diet Book* (*see Reading List, page 239*).

A regular lifestyle

This is essential for all of us if we wish to have good health (*see Chapter 8, page 203*), but it is especially important for someone who has diabetes. Eating regularly, sleeping regular hours and getting regular exercise have all been found to increase the sugar control of a diabetic and thus increase health.

Exercise

Moderate exercise has been found to be beneficial to a diabetic. Exercise keeps the blood vessels healthier, reducing risks of circulation problems. Exercise is best done on a regular basis (*see Chapter 4 for more on exercise*).

Overwork and rest

Chinese medicine suggests that often people who become diabetic have weakened their energy by overworking for long periods. It is important for those with diabetes to take regular rest breaks during the day, including after meals, and to eat meals slowly and in restful conditions.

Sex

Chinese medicine also cites too much sex as a precipitating factor for diabetes. If someone is overworking they can develop a large sexual appetite as a way to help the body to release stress. This can lead to depletion of the Qi, especially of the Kidneys.

Emotions

An emotional shock can be the precipitating factor before the onset of diabetes. Keeping healthy generally can enable a person to deal with emotional shocks and crises if they arise. Remaining emotionally balanced can help someone who has diabetes to keep their sugar well-controlled (*see Chapter 3 page 61 for more on keeping balanced emotionally*).

Chinese medicine treatment

A and CH.

It is unlikely that a person with Type 1 diabetes will be able to come off insulin completely even with acupuncture or Chinese herbal treatment. A person with Type 2 diabetes who takes tablets may be able to reduce them with the help of these treatments. Treatment can be useful to supplement a healthy regime and help a person with diabetes to maintain their health.

Diarrhea

Chinese medicine diagnosis

It is normal to pass a well-formed stool every day. If the stools are semi-formed or watery and we open our bowels more than once or twice a day then we have diarrhea. If we have chronic diarrhea we will not get enough nourishment from our food. Long-term this weakens our Qi.

Chinese medicine finds many causes for diarrhea. The most common ones are:

Deficient Spleen Qi

The Spleen rules our digestion and is responsible for moving and transforming our food and drink. If the Spleen becomes weak it is no longer able to transform and move our food. This causes the food to pass straight through the intestines causing diarrhea.

Dampness

Dampness can be compared to muddy water stuck inside us. It can block the Spleen's ability to move and transform our food and drink. Sometimes the Damp can be combined with Cold in the body, causing a watery stool and some abdominal pain. Damp can also combine with Heat and the stool then has a strong odor and is watery and yellow.

Stagnant Liver Qi combined with a weak Spleen

This is often caused and made worse by worry, nervousness, anger and anxiety.

Lifestyle changes which may prevent or improve diarrhea

Diet

One of the most common causes of loose bowels is too much Cold food in our diet. The Chinese say that the Spleen likes 'warmth'. If we eat too much Cold food the Spleen can't work efficiently and our food is not digested well. Cold food includes any food which is eaten straight from the fridge such as iced drinks, ice cream or yogurts. It is better to take food or drink at room temperature. Cold food also includes fruits which are Cold in nature and too many raw vegetables which can also be hard to digest. For more on Cold food see Chapter 2, page 35. See also a list of foods which are Cold in nature and Warm foods which can be used as a substitute.

Excessive amounts of sweet food can also weaken the Spleen and this can exacerbate loose bowels (*see Chapter 2 page 37*).

People who are prone to diarrhea can strengthen their Spleen energy by eating regularly and taking a healthy diet with the correct proportions of grains and vegetables and only small quantities of rich foods. Cutting down on Phlegm and Damp-forming foods such as dairy produce can also benefit those who have loose bowels. It is best to avoid fast food or other poor quality food as these weaken the Spleen.

Acute, extremely foul smelling diarrhea is sometimes caused by eating too much greasy Hot food and heating food such as strong curries or excessive fatty meat such as lamb or beef. Acute diarrhea can also be caused by eating unclean food – we should take care to observe proper food hygiene.

Climatic causes

Loose bowels can be caused by excessive Cold, Heat or Dampness. It is often fashionable during hot summer weather to leave the stomach and abdomen uncovered by wearing a bikini or a short blouse. If this area is unprotected and the weather becomes cold then the Cold can penetrate the stomach and abdomen causing acute and painful diarrhea. If we walk around in bare feet the Cold can travel up the legs to the intestines causing acute diarrhea. Sitting on damp grass can allow Dampness to directly penetrate the lower abdomen causing loose bowels.

Emotions

If we are worried or slightly stressed for a short time we can have an episode of loose bowels which clears once the stress is cleared. If we are under constant stress in our home or work situation this can result in chronic diarrhea which can be very depleting. By dealing with the cause of the stress our diarrhea can be eliminated. For more on our emotions see Chapter 3, page 52.

Overwork or overactivity

If we constantly work for long hours without rest or if we overexercise we will deplete our Spleen Qi and cause loose bowels. If we have chronic loose bowels we can benefit from eating in restful conditions and taking a short nap after eating. This will help the Spleen to transform our food so that it can nourish us.

Chinese medicine treatment

A, CH and TM.

Headaches

Chinese medicine diagnosis

There are many types of headaches. They can occur on different parts of the head, have varying types of pain and be experienced at a range of intensities. One simple way of classifying headaches is to notice whether they are 'full' in their nature or 'empty'.

A 'full' headache

This is often described as throbbing, boring, stabbing, pulling, distending, or heavy. These pains are often severe and the headache can be very debilitating. Chinese medicine teaches that these headaches often arise from overactive functioning of the Liver but they can also be caused by Dampness. The headaches are varied and can be situated on the temples, at the sides or top of the head or behind the eyes. A headache from Dampness can create a heavy feeling on the forehead.

A 'deficient' headache

This is often described as a weak, dull or empty headache. Deficient headaches are often due to deficient Qi especially of the Kidneys or can be due to Blood deficiency. The pain is less intense and is often an empty feeling inside the head, or is at the back of the neck, on the forehead or at the top of the head.

Lifestyle changes which may prevent or improve headaches

The two most common triggers for headaches are diet and stress, although general lifestyle can also be important.

Diet

Diet can play an important part in helping to relieve headaches. Some headaches are exacerbated by one food. We can use this simple method to find out if a food is causing headaches or is making them worse:

1 choose one or two foods which are frequently taken in the diet and stop eating them for a period of four to six weeks
2 notice if the frequency of the headaches reduces during this time

3 if the headaches do not reduce start eating the foods again and choose one or two new foods to stop eating for a further four to six weeks
4 we can continue isolating different foods until we have found the major triggers.

The most common triggers for headaches cited by Western doctors are cheese, chocolate and oranges and it is indeed a good idea for anyone who has headaches to try cutting these foods from their diet. Coffee and tea can also set off headaches and anyone who drinks alcohol should try cutting it from their diet. Alcohol is very 'Hot' in its nature and it can cause a headache from too much 'Heat' going to the head. Heating foods such as curries and red meats can also cause headaches.

A diet full of rich and greasy food or Phlegm and Damp-forming food can be the cause of headaches due to Damp. This may result in a heavy feeling across the forehead. A dull headache on the forehead or at the top of the head can be caused by Blood deficiency. For those who are vegetarian, a diet which contains animal protein may help stop the headaches. Those who don't wish to eat meat need to be especially careful to have a diet rich in Blood nourishing food (*see Chapter 2, page 27 for dietary hints for vegetarians*).

A poor quality diet or not eating enough food can also be the cause of headaches, so anyone who has headaches is advised to make sure they eat well and at regular intervals.

Emotions and stress

A headache is often a 'message' that we are under stress. Pent-up frustration and anger, excessive worrying, anxiety or fear can all be the cause of headaches. If our emotions are unexpressed over a period of time they can build up until they explode into a headache. Some women get headaches before a period when they are most tense. Other people find that they get headaches after the source of stress is over and when they are resting. This often occurs at the weekend.

Those who are prone to headaches caused by stress need to isolate the cause of the tension. Once they discover which situations can provoke a headache they can avoid the trigger as much as possible and also deal with the underlying cause (*see Chapter 3 for dealing with our emotions*).

Too much mental work

People who are in jobs where they have to think or concentrate for long periods of time can be prone to headaches. This includes people who are studying, working with computers, or those who do large amounts of reading. Eye or neck strain caused by the mental work can also cause a headache. Anyone involved in this kind of mental work is advised to take five-minute rest breaks every hour. Gently rotating the neck in clockwise and anti-clockwise circles will help to reduce neck strain and also relaxes the eyes.

Overwork or too much exercise

Excessive overworking can weaken our Qi energy and/or our Blood and cause headaches. If we notice that our headaches come on or intensify when we work harder then we might need to cut down on what we are doing.

Chinese medicine treatment

A, CM and TM.

Hypertension

Chinese medicine diagnosis

Headaches, dizziness, irritability or a slight ringing in the ears are all signals of high blood pressure. More often people don't have any obvious signs and symptoms. They often discover that their blood pressure is high when they have it measured by a Western doctor. Long-term chronic high blood pressure can cause a stroke or a heart attack. Chinese medicine teaches that the main causes of high blood pressure are:

Overactivity of the 'Yang' energy

Yang energy moves and warms us, whilst Yin energy cools and settles us down. If our Yang energy is overactive this can raise the blood pressure.

Phlegm

This can fur up the arteries and is similar to arteriosclerosis in Western medicine.

Deficient Kidney Qi

Weakened functioning of the Kidney energy can also cause hypertension.

Lifestyle changes which may prevent or improve hypertension

Common lifestyle causes of hypertension are a combination of stress, diet and lack of rest and relaxation. If people learn to deal with these areas they can often successfully lower their blood pressure.

Warning: People on blood pressure tablets should only cut them down under the guidance of their doctor.

Emotional stress

Stress which causes a person to become frustrated, resentful or explosively angry can be a major reason for hypertension and may cause the 'Yang' energy to become overactive. Finding ways to deal with the angry feelings can be essential in reducing blood pressure. For more on dealing with our emotions, see Chapter 3, particularly page 66.

Diet

Too much rich, fatty food in the diet is a common cause of high blood pressure. Cutting out Phlegm and Damp-forming food especially dairy produce such as milk, butter and cheese, as well as fatty meat products and any other rich food such as mayonnaise, ice cream, and rich cakes and biscuits can help to lower the blood pressure.

Salt

People with a high salt intake are also advised to cut down. Salt regulates the water balance in the body but in large quantities it will stress the heart and kidneys and intensify high blood pressure.

Alcohol

Alcohol is very Heating and over consumption can create too much Heat in the body. This can in turn raise the blood pressure. For those who are drinking on a daily basis, cutting down or cutting out alcohol can help to lower the blood pressure.

Relaxation

Anything which relaxes a person will help to bring down their blood pressure. This could include meditation, relaxation exercises or listening to relaxing music. Some people find that buying a relaxation tape enables them to unwind and rest and this in turn helps to lower the blood pressure (*see Chapter 4 for more on rest*). Gentle exercises such as Qigong and Tai Ji Quan can also be beneficial.

Overwork

Overworking can put the body under such strain that it raises blood pressure. In this case the hypertension is a signal to reassess the way that we are working and to relax more.

Chinese medicine treatment

A, CH and TM.

Indigestion and Heartburn

Chinese medicine diagnosis

Symptoms of indigestion include discomfort and/or pain in the stomach, feeling full, sour regurgitation or belching. Indigestion is most commonly due to:

Food stagnating in the stomach
The Liver Qi becoming Stagnant

In both of these cases the normal digestive process has temporarily stopped.

Lifestyle changes which may prevent or improve indigestion and heartburn

The main causes of indigestion are an overly rich diet, overeating, unexpressed anger or worry.

Diet

Anyone who frequently gets indigestion is advised to examine their diet (*see Chapter 2, page 18 for the proportions of food in the diet*). If the diet contains too high a percentage of rich food then reducing this to 10–15 per cent can help to alleviate the problem. Indigestion can also be caused by overeating, in which case the diet needs to be modified.

Those who get indigestion can also strive to eat in situations which are as stress-free and as calm as possible and to continue to relax for a little while after eating in order to aid the digestive process.

Emotions

If we are gripped by anxiety, fear, worry or dread it can affect the solar plexus and stomach. This may cause the digestive process to come to a temporary standstill.

Unexpressed anger and resentment can also cause our digestion to slow down or come to a standstill. Once the problem has been resolved, digestion will start moving again. A person with long-term resentment or anger which has not been resolved may get chronic indigestion. In this case the feelings may be resolved when the person learns to forgive and let go of their negative feelings.

Some people with digestive problems find themselves in situations which they find hard to sort out and 'digest'. In this case they may need to observe the situation closely in order to find the best way to deal with it and 'digest' it thoroughly. For more on dealing with our emotions see Chapter 3, page 61.

Chinese medicine treatment

A, CH and TM.

Chinese herbs travel directly to the gut. In some cases this may be beneficial and treatment may help us to digest food better. In other cases acupuncture or Tuina massage may be preferable treatment as they by-pass the digestion and work directly on our Qi.

Insomnia

Chinese medicine diagnosis

Insomnia is the inability to get off to sleep or waking in the night having initially fallen asleep. The three most common causes of insomnia are:

Blood deficiency

This will often cause a person to have difficulty falling asleep at night. Blood deficiency causes the Spirit to become unsettled. The unsettled feeling will then cause the person to remain awake at night instead of sleeping.

Yin deficiency

Insomnia can arise when the calming and cooling Yin energy is deficient. This causes a person to wake up for periods in the middle of the night – often having got off to sleep without any difficulty.

Heat

Someone who is too Hot inside may have difficulty sleeping or may wake for periods during the night.

Lifestyle changes which may prevent or improve insomnia

Emotions

Many of us have the occasional time when we go to bed worried, anxious or angry and find we can't sleep. If this happens frequently it is time to examine our lifestyle and deal with the cause of our emotional upsets. Anxiety and worry are dealt with earlier in this chapter but for more on dealing with our emotions generally see Chapter 3, page 61.

Overwork and rest

Many people who overwork, especially in a stressful environment, find that when they go to bed they can't sleep. Before going to bed we need to make sure that we have wound down so that we are relaxed. We can do this by going for a quiet walk, having a relaxing bath, listening to a relaxation tape, meditating or doing any other restful activity. We also need to make sure we don't overstimulate ourselves before bed by carrying out activities such as strenuous exercise, watching a scary film or reading overstimulating books. See Chapter 4, page 104 for more on insomnia and page 106 for a Qigong exercise to practice before sleeping.

Diet

Eating irregularly or late at night can cause insomnia by putting a strain on the stomach and intestines which are having to digest food when they should be resting. People who overeat on a regular basis can also find it difficult to sleep. Eating too much rich food such as puddings and sweets can make a person unable to sleep.

Too much Hot food such as curries, red meats or alcohol can overheat a person and cause insomnia. For vegetarians, adding some meat to the diet can help to nourish the Blood and settle the Spirit.

Caffeine

People who drink large amounts of coffee, tea and colas can find that the caffeine prevents them sleeping. Cutting down or cutting out these drinks and replacing them with herb teas, coffee substitutes or hot water can also help induce sleep.

Sleeping times

People who have insomnia are advised to go to bed at a regular time every night. Our bodies then get into the habit of preparing to sleep at this time. One old wives' tale tells us that the hours before midnight are twice as beneficial to us as the hours after midnight. Rest and sleep are vital for our well-being and getting to bed well before midnight will ensure that we get nourishing sleep.

Posture and direction

Sleeping on our back or on our right side will take the pressure off our internal organs. This will prevent illness later in life (*see Chapter 5, page 103*). Sleeping with the head pointing towards the north will often help us to sleep more deeply as we are then aligned to the earth's magnetic field.

Blood loss

Blood loss from heavy periods (sometimes as a result of using a coil) or following an accident or labor can cause Blood deficiency. This causes the Spirit to become restless, creating insomnia. Eating a healthy diet full of Blood nourishing foods will help to remedy this. The Chinese especially suggest chicken after giving birth. If the blood loss is due to using the coil then it may be important to change the type of contraception used.

Chinese medicine treatment
A and CH.

Joint Problems

Chinese medicine diagnosis

Chinese medicine views joint pain in a different way from Western medicine. Joint pains can be caused by both a 'full' condition or 'deficient' condition. Often they are caused by the climatic factors of Wind, Cold, Damp, Heat and also Phlegm. In this case they are 'full'. If there is Blood deficiency or the Qi is weak, then the joint pains are 'deficient'.

'Full' joint pains
Wind in the joints is characterized by pain in the muscles and joints which moves from place to place. *Cold* in the joints causes severe pain which creates limitation of movement.

Dampness in the joints is characterized by stiffness and swelling along with a feeling of heaviness in the joint or limb.

Heat in the joints causes them to become red, swollen, hot and painful.

When the joints have been affected for a long period of time the fluids dry up causing nodules to form. Chinese medicine calls these *'Phlegm' nodules*.

'Deficient' joint pains
If our Qi and Blood is deficient this can cause the joints to be achy rather than painful. The limbs may also feel weak.

The heading 'joint pains' covers a large number of conditions which include rheumatoid arthritis, osteo-arthritis, bursitis, fibrositis, injured joints etc.

An injury to a joint or a joint which is 'worn out' will affect only one joint at a time. Inflamed joints such as those found in rheumatoid arthritis are more severe and several joints will be affected.

Lifestyle changes which may prevent or improve joint conditions

Protection from the environment

Wind, Cold or Damp can enter the body from the outside. Those who already have joint problems caused by Wind, Damp, Cold etc. are often more susceptible to the External climate.

Those with Damp in their joints will often be vulnerable to damp or humid weather. People with this condition often know when the weather is turning damp because of the achy feeling they experience. In the same way, Wind or Cold can also exacerbate joint pains. Extremely hot weather can also worsen red hot swollen joints.

We can protect ourselves from these climatic conditions as much as possible by wearing appropriate clothing and living in a healthy environment. For more on the secret of protection from the environment see Chapter 5.

Diet

Diet can have a beneficial effect on the joints. Eating a healthy diet which is rich in fresh vegetables and fruit as well as grains and beans with only a small amount of fat can help to strengthen us so that we are no longer weakened by our condition.

We can also notice if our joints seem to be more Damp, Hot or Cold. We can then cut out excessively hot or cold foods or any rich or Phlegm and Damp-forming foods accordingly (*see Chapter 2, pages 22 and 35*). Drinking excessive amounts of orange juice can also exacerbate some joint conditions.

Trauma

An injury to a joint may be the precursor to a later joint problem. Anyone with an injured joint is advised to make sure it is rested and heals properly before it is used again. An injury which doesn't heal completely is vulnerable to the climatic factors of Wind, Cold and Damp. These can easily enter an injured joint causing arthritis later on in life.

Emotions

An emotional crisis or shock can trigger arthritis. The trigger can be the death of a loved one, redundancy, divorce or financial problems or any other life crisis. Often this kind of shock will cause a large number of joints to be-come inflamed. We can't tell when a crisis is coming our way and the best way to guard against the worst effects of this kind of situation is to keep as healthy as possible. We can do this by eating, sleeping and resting regularly and by keeping a positive attitude to life as much as possible.

Exercise

Regular, gentle exercise such as Tai Ji Quan or Qigong is often beneficial to our joints and can help our mobility. It will also strengthen our underlying Qi which can be weakened by the arthritic condition. These exercises are gentle and don't strain the joints. Vigorous exercise such as running or play-ing racket games can strain the joints and will not be of benefit to people who have arthritic conditions or joint problems.

Swimming can often be helpful to someone with joint pains as the water protects the joints while they are exercised. If someone has Damp or Cold in the joints, however, the person should guard against getting cold when leav-ing the pool or not drying themselves properly as this can sometimes cause further 'invasions' of Cold and Damp. For more on protection from the envi-ronment see Chapter 5, page 111.

Rest

Some joint problems are caused by overuse of one particular area. For example someone who is constantly carrying heavy loads may be affected in the hips. A footballer may get bad knees. A typist may get problems with the hands and wrists – a symptom commonly known as Repetitive Strain Injury or RSI. If one area is affected by overuse then it is advisable to rest this area as much as possible so that it can heal. This may prevent further problems arising in the future. A change of job may even be necessary if the problem does not subside.

Chinese medicine treatment
A, TM and CH.

In China, acupuncture or Tuina massage are often the first treatments used by people with joint conditions. Treatment can be very successful. Chinese herbs can also be helpful.

Menopausal Hot Flushes

Chinese medicine diagnosis

Depletion of the 'Yin' energy

This is the most common cause of menopausal hot flushes. Yin is cooling, moisturizing and calming. Yang on the other hand is heating, drying and moving. As we grow older we need to rest appropriately. Many of us continue to overwork when we need to rest and this uses up the Yin energy. We are left with too little of this Cooling energy and too much Hot energy, causing hot flushes.

Lifestyle changes which may prevent or improve menopausal hot flushes

It may be useful for women who have hot flushes to keep a journal of situations that have occurred just prior to the hot flush. This will then enable them to understand what has triggered the flush. Triggers are often one or more of the things listed below.

Overwork and rest

It is now normal for many people to overwork in ways they never did before. Overwork can wear out our Yin energy. Hot flushes when they first appear can be a signal to us that we need to rest. If we take notice of this signal and really take it easy the flushes will often reduce in their intensity. It is interesting to note that hot flushes are not as common in China as in the West. This may change as the Chinese people's lifestyle becomes more Westernized. Resting may involve cutting down on work, getting enough sleep or finding ways to relax such as meditation or relaxation exercises.

Diet

For those who are getting hot flushes it is best to avoid eating too many Heating foods. These include red meats such as beef and lamb, curries, alcohol and coffee.

Stress and emotions

Repressed emotions such as anger and frustration can result in a build-up of Heat in the body. If these emotions are discharged a person may feel able to 'cool off' and the flushes may then reduce in frequency.

Climate

A hot climate although not usually the cause of hot flushes can exacerbate them so that they intensify. People who have hot flushes should avoid situations where they will be hot for long periods. These include working in hot kitchens, going away to very hot climates or having saunas. If the heat is unavoidable then it is best to protect ourselves as much as possible by wearing cotton clothes which allow us to sweat and to wear a hat to protect the head from the sun.

Chinese medicine treatment

A and CH.

Period Pains

Chinese medicine diagnosis

Chinese medicine describes many different types of period pains. The main ones are:

Cold in the lower abdomen

Pains from Cold are sharp and 'biting' in their nature. These are often better with the application of heat.

Stagnation of Qi in the lower abdomen

Period pains which have a distended (bloated) feeling will often be due to stagnation of the Qi in the lower abdomen. Rubbing the stuck area will encourage the Qi to move and help to alleviate the pain.

Stagnation of Blood in the lower abdomen

Some period pains are extremely intense and do not easily respond to any massage or heat. These may be accompanied by blood clots. They are often due to Blood which is stuck in the lower abdomen.

187

Lifestyle changes which may prevent or improve period pains

Protection from the environment

We can protect ourselves against Cold or Damp conditions by not sitting on stone steps – this may cause Cold and Damp to enter the lower abdomen. We can also avoid leaving the abdomen uncovered and always wear shoes or slippers when walking on cold floors. Some young girls playing sports at school have to stand in cold fields wearing only shorts. Cold can then enter the lower abdomen causing period pains due to cold. For more details on protection from the environment see Chapter 5, page 111.

If the period pains are caused by Cold in the lower abdomen then the application of heat will help temporarily. A hot water bottle or hot pad can be placed over the site of the pain.

Sex

It is best to avoid sex during the period as the uterus is at its most fragile and is more susceptible to the climate, especially to the Cold. The Cold can then cause period pains.

Massage

Rubbing the abdomen will usually help to lessen period pains which are caused by Qi Stagnation. This helps to get the Qi moving and in turn moves the pain.

Diet

If the period pains are due to cold in the lower abdomen, then it is best to avoid Cold food. This includes iced drinks or food taken straight from the fridge, salad and raw food, and cold fruits. Add more Warming foods to the diet by taking a moderate amount of meat and eating other Hot food such as a small amount of ginger added to hot water or porridge. For a list of the temperatures of food see Chapter 2, page 35.

Stress

Living or working in a situation which is stressful can exacerbate period pains especially those caused by Qi Stagnation. Often factors such as Cold, stress and diet can all combine to intensify the condition. For those who recognize that emotions play a large part in their discomfort, dealing with the cause of the stress may be the first step to alleviating the pain (*see Chapter 3, page 52 for more on the emotions*).

Chinese medicine treatment
A, CH and TM.

Period pains due to Blood stagnation are extreme pains which may not respond to a change in lifestyle. In this case it is best to seek acupuncture or Chinese herbal medicine. Other types of period pains will also respond to the Chinese treatments. The lifestyle changes suggested will then keep the pains from recurring.

Post-viral Syndrome

Chinese medicine diagnosis

Post-viral syndrome or Myalgic Encephalomyelitis commonly known as ME is now a frequent cause of chronic illness. These conditions are usually caused by a combination of:

Wind, Cold, Heat or Damp
The Wind enters the body usually in combination with Cold, Heat or Damp. This causes an infection – usually labeled a 'virus' by Western medicine. The infection then remains in the body especially in the form of Damp or Heat.

Qi and Blood deficiency
The Qi and Blood is too weak to expel the infection. This usually results in a person remaining in a collapsed state.

A person with post-viral syndrome can experience a large variety of symptoms including muscle fatigue and aches, poor memory and concentration, exhaustion and a persisting, intermittent flu-like feeling.

Lifestyle changes which may prevent or improve post-viral syndrome

Prevention

The best 'treatment' for post-viral syndrome is prevention. People who get this condition are often chronically overworking and weakening their body's energy. If they then catch an infection resulting in an invasion of Wind, Cold, Heat or Damp they are not strong enough to throw it off. Proper rest during an illness and then taking time to convalesce will give the body the chance to regain its strength so that it can throw off the climatic factor/virus.

To prevent post-viral syndrome it is advisable to live a lifestyle which is not overly stressful or overactive. We can also rest when we are tired and eat nourishing food.

For a person who has got post-viral syndrome, a healthy lifestyle is essential. They are also advised to seek the help of an acupuncturist, Chinese herbalist or Tuina massage practitioner to strengthen the body further.

Rest

Rest is essential to prevent post-viral syndrome. Once someone has this condition, they feel so worn out, it is impossible not to rest. Many people with this condition can't accept their change in circumstances and some find they are too restless to relax properly. Acceptance can be one of the first steps to recovery.

Diet

Eating a well-proportioned diet with very little rich food and lots of grains and vegetables is strengthening to the body. Often eliminating Phlegm and Damp-forming foods from the diet (*see Chapter 2, page 22*) and if there is Heat in the system, cutting down on heating foods (*see Chapter 2, page 35*) can help to clear Damp or Heat from the body and help recovery.

Caffeine

Some people with post-viral conditions find that cutting out caffeinated drinks such as coffee, teas, hot chocolate and colas will help to improve the condition. Caffeinated drinks make us edgy and restless, which stops us from fully resting so that we can recover.

Avoid getting infections

Avoiding getting infections by protecting ourselves from extremes of Wind, Cold, Damp and Heat or changes in temperature can be important to both prevent and alleviate post-viral conditions. If a person has a post-viral condition the body may be too weak to fight an infection. The climatic cause merely gets stuck inside the body making the condition worse.

Light exercise

Chinese exercises such as Qigong or Tai Qi Quan can be beneficial to a person who has post-viral syndrome. They can often help to clear the Wind, Cold, Damp or Heat from the system. Light walking, or short sessions of other light exercises can also be helpful. It is best to avoid strenuous exercise as this will weaken the Qi and Blood.

Stress and emotions

People who are ill with post-viral syndromes have often been leading a highly stressful life before getting sick. Once ill, the condition itself becomes an additional stressor and the person often feels impatient to get better. As post-viral symptoms can linger for long periods of time it can be essential for people to accept the situation they are in and to use it as a time to re-examine their previous way of life. They can then make any necessary modifications to their lifestyle to assist the healing process and enable them to remain healthy in the future.

Chinese medicine treatment

A, CM and TM.

Lifestyle is a major factor in the treatment of post-viral syndrome. As stated above, Chinese herbal medicine, acupuncture or Tuina massage can also be important to support the healing process.

Premenstrual Syndrome

Chinese medicine diagnosis

The main symptoms of this condition are fluctuating moods, depression or anger before the period, tender or swollen breasts and a swollen abdomen. Women usually begin to feel premenstrual three to four days before their period begins. Sometimes premenstrual tension can start as early as two weeks before a period. In this case it is very debilitating. The main cause of premenstrual syndrome is:

Stagnation of the Liver Qi

The Liver is responsible for the smooth and even movement of Qi throughout the body. If the Liver is not smoothing the Qi it moves unevenly, causing us to feel erratic, angry and irritable, as well as having the other symptoms described above.

Lifestyle changes which may prevent or improve premenstrual syndrome

Stress and emotions

Those who have premenstrual syndrome may notice that additional difficulties during the preceding month can worsen the premenstrual symptoms. If on the other hand the month tends to run smoothly then the premenstrual tension is better. Whatever is happening either exacerbates or alleviates the quality of the premenstrual tension. Dealing with any unresolved issues in our lives can be essential to lessening the effects of this condition (*see Chapter 3 on dealing with emotions*).

Rest

Taking a rest for half an hour every day can help to relax a person. This allows the Liver Qi to move and can help to clear premenstrual conditions.

Cut out tea and coffee

Caffeinated drinks can cause us to become overtense and agitated, so cutting out caffeinated drinks can help to lessen the effects of premenstrual syndrome.

Exercise

Light exercise gets the Qi moving and can have a profound effect on clearing Qi stagnation. Gentle exercises such as Qigong or Tai Ji Quan can be helpful as well as brisk walking, swimming, dancing and other sports.

Chinese medicine treatment

A, CH and TM.

Skin Conditions

Chinese medicine diagnosis

There are many different skin conditions – eczema, psoriasis, herpes zoster, dermatitis and urticaria to name a few. It is not within the capacity of this book to go into diagnostic details of every one of these conditions nor is it necessary. A general Chinese diagnosis can be made by observing the skin.

Most skin conditions are a combination of an underlying weakness in our Qi and/or Blood and External causes such as Wind, Cold, Damp or Heat affecting the skin:

Wind

This will cause rashes which move around and come and go. These can be itchy and bleed, then scabs will form and they will heal up and go away again.

Damp

This causes discharges, blisters and suppuration from the skin; there can also be puffy skin and swelling.

Heat

This creates red, raised, painful skin conditions with a clear margin between the good skin and the diseased skin.

Cold

This creates pale colored skin conditions which are better with heat.

Blood deficiency

This underlies many skin conditions. The main symptoms will be dry and flaky skin.

Qi deficiency

General weakness of Qi will affect the skin but especially deficiency of the Lung Qi. The Chinese teach that the Lung and skin are connected. If the Lung Qi is weak this may cause many skin conditions.

Lifestyle changes which may prevent or improve skin conditions

Diet and emotions are the two most common causes of skin conditions.

Diet

A change in diet can often make a great difference to skin problems. We can adjust diet according to what kind of skin condition is present and we can also identify any individual foods which may trigger the skin problem.

Anyone who has a skin problem is advised to consider the proportions of foods which are taken in their diet. If it is full of extremely rich food, including spicy food, overly sweet food or fatty food then it is advisable to find a better balance in the diet. It is also advisable to eat plenty of freshly cooked vegetables.

If a skin problem is due to Heat then it is best to avoid Heating foods in the diet. These include lamb and other red meats, alcohol, and hot curries which will heat the skin further (*see Chapter 2 page 35 for a list of the temperature of food*). Many sea foods such as mussels, lobsters, shrimps and prawns are Warm in their temperature and can trigger Hot skin conditions. Those who have a Hot skin condition can add slightly Cooling foods to the diet but not in excess.

If a skin problem is due to Dampness then it is sensible to cut out or cut down on Phlegm and Damp-forming foods, especially dairy produce and fatty foods (*see Chapter 2, page 22 for a list of Phlegm and Damp-forming foods*).

Blood moistens the skin. Dry skin which is often found in eczema and psoriasis can be due to a deficiency of Blood. In this case a healthy diet rich in Blood nourishing food can help to lessen the Blood deficiency and will in time benefit the skin.

A skin condition can be triggered by one or two foods taken in the diet. To ascertain which food is causing the problem cut out the suspected foods for a few weeks and notice if the skin condition starts to abate.

Emotions

Unresolved emotional problems start to make us feel uncomfortable. If this discomfort is not resolved it may begin to reflect in our skin. Strong emotions especially anger can cause Heat in the body and can create red raised painful skin conditions. Anxiety and worry can result from Blood deficiency and create dry or flaky skin. As stated earlier the Chinese say that the skin is the manifestation of the Lungs. Grief is the emotion connected to the Lung and unexpressed grief can also result in skin problems. For more on the emotions see Chapter 3, page 52.

Climate

Externally Hot situations including hot baths can exacerbate Hot skin conditions and Cold skin problems can feel worse in cold weather. The skin protects us from the outside elements and if the Lung's Wei Qi or defensive Qi is weak the climatic causes can easily penetrate beneath the surface of the skin contributing to skin conditions. For more on protection from the climate, see Chapter 5, page 111.

Chinese medicine treatment
A and CH.

Skin conditions can be treated by any of the Chinese treatments but Chinese herbs are certainly the most tried and tested remedy. They often have a remarkable effect. It is often best to combine lifestyle adjustments with Chinese herbal treatments for the care of many skin conditions, especially severe cases.

This chapter has provided lifestyle suggestions for many common conditions. Even if your complaint is not mentioned in this chapter, following the guiding principles written in the main text of the book will enable you to discover how to live more healthily. In the next chapter we will look at how to start on our journey to better health.

Where do I Start?

Having read this book you may now feel inspired to make adjustments to your lifestyle. Like any worthwhile changes these adjustments may require some planning.

A patient recently told me:

> I know I need to make some changes to my lifestyle but when I think about it I get overwhelmed and confused so I end up doing nothing. I then continue with the same old bad habits.

Another said:

> I wish I could make permanent changes. I start with good intentions and completely turn my life around for a while, but then it all falls apart and I go back to what I did before.

Planning our adjustments

Failure to plan can result in a failure to make long lasting changes. That's why when we are making significant changes for ourselves it is best to approach them with the same care and forethought as we would put into a wedding, career change, or finding our dream home.

My advice to anyone wishing to make alterations to their lifestyle is:

1 become motivated to make modifications to your lifestyle
2 find ways to make changes as enjoyable as possible
3 make changes at the speed you want to make them
4 turn any changes into regular good habits.

We'll look at each of these in turn.

Find Ways to Become Motivated

If we wish to improve our health we need to become motivated to make the necessary alterations. Some people may have read this book and found that they become strongly motivated to improve their lifestyle as they read it. So how did this happen?

Motivation stems from looking ahead and imagining either the positive results of our actions or the negative consequences of not taking action. If these are compelling enough to us we become motivated to make changes.

The positive consequences

One common positive result of changing our lifestyle is a greater sense of well-being. This has consistently been found in many studies. An article from the journal *American Health* cited the psychological effects of exercise. Swimmers reported feeling more vigor and significantly less levels of depression after spending 30–60 minutes in a pool and walkers who were formerly overweight who spent 45 minutes a day walking five days a week reported improvements in mood. They also had an overall feeling of well-being that extended to other areas of their lives.[1]

Other positive consequences of altering our lifestyle include a clearer mind, better concentration, greater contentment, consistent energy, relaxed muscles, a feeling of internal calmness, brighter spirits, a good appetite, better weight control, clear skin, bright eyes, glossy hair, flexible joints, regular bowels, strong teeth and good vitality.

I'm sure you can think of many other benefits you could gain...

The negative consequences

What about the negative consequences of failing to make changes? Some of these might be depression, lack of energy, constipation, inertia, weight gain, flabby muscles, stiff joints, anxiety, constant coughs and colds, loose bowels, poor sleep, poor memory, lack of appetite, constantly getting upset, irritability or general failing health.

The 'carrot' and the 'stick'

Most of us need both a positive and a negative payoff together to be truly compelled to change. Here Sue, who was recovering from breast cancer, puts it simply:

> I had no option but to change my lifestyle, I had become ill and now I really wanted to enjoy my life and be healthy.

Pam, a colleague, was motivated for both negative and positive reasons:

> I am a mother, a wife and a practitioner and I need to stay healthy in order to have energy and the presence of mind to do these things. By experiencing the negative consequences of my lifestyle I realized what wasn't for me. At the same time I had to set realistic health goals and not become rigid or obsessed with my lifestyle.

To motivate ourselves we should consider the consequences of our actions on our future health.

Looking ahead

First, consider what could be the positive consequences for you if you alter your lifestyle. Next, what might be the negative ones if you don't look after your health? Finally, consider your long-term as well as your short-term future and how healthy you might be in three, five or 10 years time or in the later years of your life?

You can write these discoveries down now and use them as you go through the Seven-Step Plan for Healthy Living in Chapter 9.

Knowing that others have gained positive benefits from adjusting their lifestyle can add to our motivation. Theresa told me:

> What can I say, I can't believe the change. I wish I had done it 10 years earlier.

Bob also said it was worth it:

> Along with the birth of my kids it rates as the best thing that happened to me – by far!

For most people the next suggestion is also important.

Find Ways to Make Changes as Enjoyable as Possible

Why do some of us make permanent changes to our lifestyle whilst others have good intentions which come to nothing? The answer is complex of course, our habits, upbringing and emotional predisposition all come into it. Overall, one of the strongest reasons we have for continuing to do what we do is the enjoyment factor. It is best if we have an enjoyable alternative to our unhealthy habits. We can then gain pleasure from the results.

Creative changes

Some people imagine that a healthy lifestyle is a mass of rigid rules. If we put ourselves into a strait-jacket we are doomed to fail in our attempts to make lifestyle shifts. A better option is to look for creative ways to make the changes in our lifestyle enjoyable. Modifications often involve either giving up something we do or bringing in something new.

Two methods we can use to help to make these enjoyable are:

1 finding a substitute when we give something up
2 looking for the most enjoyable option when we choose to do something new.

Finding a substitute

Substitution can be especially helpful when we are changing our diet. Soya milk can make a good substitute for cow's milk, for example. Shopping around is important. Soya milk has varying tastes according to the brand and some are much nicer than others. It is also important to eat organic to avoid GM soya.

We can also look out for different substitutes for coffee and tea. Those who decide to give up coffee may prefer not to try taking one of the coffee 'substitutes' such as Caro or Barleycup – they'll never taste like the real thing! It might be better to try out completely new tastes. We can look out for interesting herb teas – 'Lemon Zinger' or 'Revitalise tea' might take our fancy or try Rooibosh tea for a change.

Paula cut down on sugar:

> Taking less sugar was a really good decision for me and over a period of time I felt much better without it. When I first gave it up I was shocked at how much 'hidden' sugar there was in many foods. Once I started looking at the labels I realized that foods like frozen peas, pasta sauces and ketchup all had sugar in them. It became a challenge to find healthier foods and I became like a detective finding alternatives.

As well as being fun, substituting foods can add variety to what we eat and drink. A list of suggested substitutes for food and drink is on page 40.

Enjoyable options

Secondly, when we choose to do something new we can find the most enjoyable option available. For example, if we decide to exercise more we might ask ourselves, 'What exercise do I enjoy?' and 'What do I hope to get from doing it?' If we want to do gentle Qi-enhancing exercises we might decide to join a Tai Ji Quan, Yoga or Qigong class.

Theresa started to go to a Yoga class:

> I wanted to do some light exercise and decided to go to a local Yoga class. I
> go regularly now and really enjoy it. I'm much more supple in my joints and
> I've made a lot of friends too.

More active exercises include dance groups, joining a badminton class or learning a martial art. Some of us may prefer to give ourselves an enjoyable challenge such as walking to work most days if we usually go by car or taking up cycling.

When considering our emotions we can note with interest how we change as we keep a daily journal of appreciation, alternatively we may create some positive outcomes or we may notice the 'power of keeping in good humor'. We may even deliberately go to watch a funny film or to see a comedian. We can also experiment with making time for breaks and rest.

If we are used to having our lunch on the run we can decide to find pleasurable ways of giving ourselves a break. We might choose to go out to a park to eat if the weather is sunny, or go out to eat at a good restaurant or to find a different space in our workplace where we can relax and enjoy our food.

The examples above are only a few of the many ways we can make our lifestyle enjoyable. Doing things that we don't enjoy will ultimately have a negative impact whilst enjoyment in itself is conducive to our overall good health.

Make Changes at the Speed you Want to Make them

Some people choose to make lifestyle changes quickly while others make small modifications bit by bit. Many people make a combination of changes – some dramatic shifts then a number of slow changes.

Sue (who had breast cancer) commented:

> It was easy to do, but some changes took longer than others, diet was quick
> and I just let go of bad working habits. Rest is improving now but was
> difficult for a while as I was studying. Caring for myself has generally evolved
> over the last three years.

For many people slow changes create the most lasting results. Pat, who lives in Wales, took a number of years:

> Over a five-year period I first changed my diet, then changed my job and later took up Qigong exercises. I've also moved from town to country in the last couple of years. Living at a slower pace and closer to natural things has probably been the icing on the cake!

Prioritizing changes

As we go through the Seven-Step Plan for Healthy Living in Chapter 9, most of us will find that some alterations are easier to make than others. Often it is best to make the simplest changes first. For example, we can easily protect ourselves from the environment by wearing a scarf, changing out of wet clothes, or wearing slippers. We might choose to change these things immediately. Others, like getting enough rest, changing our diet or exercising regularly, can take a longer time to shift.

Mark told me:

> The way I changed varied, I changed my diet bit by bit, then other things have gradually filtered in as I've become comfortable with them.

Making shifts too rapidly can sometimes mean that we give up and return to our previous bad habits. In this case taking time to change may be our best course of action. We know that the Chinese understand that balance is important in everything we do. Making changes that are extreme will tend to rebound on us. We can then easily find ourselves going back to square one. The 70 per cent rule about exercising (*see page 90*) is also true of all other areas of our lifestyle.

Whatever the speed of the changes we make the next stage is to turn them into regular lifelong habits.

Turn any Changes into Regular Good Habits

Most of us are creatures of habit and it is better to have a habitual lifestyle than to live a chaotic one. Good habits are much better than bad ones.

A study was carried out by Dr Lester Breslow on 7,000 people from the 1960s to the present day at the University of California School of Public Health.[2]

The importance of regularity

Dr Breslow found that many unhealthy lifestyle practices were likely to affect a person's well-being. Some of them such as tobacco and alcohol intake were obvious, as were others such as physical inactivity. The biggest surprise, however, was the effect of an irregular lifestyle. A person who was teetotal and didn't smoke was still more likely to die prematurely or to suffer from disabling illnesses if they ate between meals, had irregular sleep or regularly skipped breakfast. Dr Breslow came to the conclusion that a regular life is one of the main ways we can maintain our health.

Besides not smoking or drinking alcohol, some of the regular good habits Dr Breslow found to affect a person's well-being were:

1 eating regular meals
2 having a good breakfast
3 getting regular moderate exercise
4 getting enough sleep
5 eating so as to maintain a moderate weight.

Joe and Freda both had irregular lifestyles which were affecting their health. Joe told me:

> I realized that in order for my health to improve I would need to make changes to what I did and the way I dealt with things. I had bowel problems and I was eating irregularly, usually late at night. I now try to eat by seven o'clock or eat a large meal at noon. I also take more regular exercise and work shorter hours. My bowels are now fine.

Freda, another patient told me:

> One of the biggest changes for me is that I now eat regular meals. I used
> to eat at eight thirty in the morning then eat nothing until three in the
> afternoon. Now I eat breakfast at eight o'clock, have lunch at one and an
> evening meal at six thirty to seven. I used to walk around and eat. Now it
> is part of my routine to sit and eat.

Simplicity

Once we decide on the alterations we wish to make, we can find ways of
bringing them into our lives so that they are effortless to continue.

One practical step is to make modifications which are so simple that they
can easily become habitual. If we then find we are getting benefit from them
we will naturally integrate them into our lives. Here are some simple changes
that Charles, Paula and Jack made that turned into good habits.

Charles said:

> I started taking food to work in a food flask instead of sandwiches and it
> made one of the biggest changes to my energy levels. When I ate little until
> the evening I was lacking energy generally and often felt quite unwell. Since
> I changed to a large cooked lunch I've had more energy especially in the latter
> part of the day and I've been emotionally and mentally stronger.

Paula had this experience:

> Before I would have driven everywhere now I walk as much as I can. I really
> enjoy the walk and feel better for it.

Finally, Jack told me:

> Having had eight bouts of tonsillitis in one year I now always look after
> myself and wear a scarf. Some people make jokes that I'd wear a scarf on
> the beach but I don't get colds any more and I haven't had tonsillitis.

By turning our lifestyle changes into good habits, we will reap the benefits and feel healthier for it. We will then feel more motivated to continue a positive cycle for lifelong good health.

It takes a month

Finally a reminder about the time it takes to create those regular good habits. Earlier in the book we discussed how it takes a month to turn the changes we make into regular good habits. Remembering this can help us to go through any discomfort we might encounter early on. We can bear in mind that difficulties will ease after the first month – following this the adjustments will become internalized and a part of our regular lifestyle.

We will be reminding ourselves of these important suggestions when we go through the Seven-Step Plan in Chapter 9. The questionnaire at the end of the book can also be used in conjunction with the Seven-Step Plan. This will enable us to find out more about our individual lifestyle needs. It's now up to each one of us to decide on which changes we wish to make.

Summary

1 It's easier to modify our lifestyle if we are motivated and if we make any adjustments as enjoyable as possible.
2 We can then change at the right speed for us and integrate any changes into our lifestyle so that they become good habits. These will help us to sustain any adjustments we make to our lifestyle.

Keeping Healthy and Preventing Disease – A Seven-Step Plan for Healthy Living

Having discussed all Five Secrets of Health and Happiness, you may already have begun to make modifications to your lifestyle. This chapter is written to enable you to focus on any other changes you wish to make. It will help you to make beneficial adjustments to your lifestyle. The plan is best read after you have completed the rest of the book.

The lifestyle questionnaire on pages 212–219 asks you general questions about your lifestyle as well as specific ones about your individual health. This is used in conjunction with the Seven-Step Plan. You may want to read through these seven steps before taking the time to do them.

Step 1

If you have not already done so, answer the questionnaire starting on page 212.

Step 2

Consider all the main health areas which you look after well, then think about those you could change to benefit your health. You can gather this information by reading the main text of the book, by filling in the Lifestyle Questionnaire or from reading any section in Chapter 7 which is relevant to you. Write these down under the three main categories.

1 The lifestyle areas which you already do well.
2 The lifestyle areas in which you sometimes do well.
3 The lifestyle areas in which you don't do at all well.

1 These areas I do well

....

....

....

....

2 These areas I sometimes do well

....

....

....

....

3 I don't do these areas well at all

....

....

....

....

Congratulate yourself on the things on the list that are in category 1. Even if you have only written one thing in this category, remind yourself that you have taken one step on the path towards a healthy lifestyle.

Step 3

Remind yourself of the four areas which are listed in Chapter 8. They will reinforce any changes you make.

1 Become motivated to make modifications to your lifestyle.
2 Find ways to make changes as enjoyable as possible.
3 Make changes at the speed you want to make them.
4 Turn any changes into regular good habits.

Now go back to Step 2 and take a look at categories 2 and 3. These are the areas you may want to change. From these lists write out the lifestyle areas which you would both like to change and could easily change NOW.

....

....

....

....

Write this list on a separate sheet and keep it in a place where you will regularly see it. This may be pinned to the wall, kept in your diary or any other place you look at frequently. Use it to remind yourself of the things you have chosen to do and DO THEM.

Congratulate yourself again! You have just taken a few more steps towards a healthy lifestyle and with very little effort! You now know which areas you are doing well in and which ones you could change with ease.

Step 4

Now look at the areas from categories 2 and 3 which might be more difficult to change. List these below:

....

....

....

....

Step 5

Take the areas you've just listed in Step 4 and prioritize them into areas which are a high priority for you to change and those which are less of a priority. For many of us there are one or two main areas that we might modify. If we altered them we would feel so much better that we could go on to change other areas. What are the main one or two areas for you? Be aware of how easily you think you can adjust them. What's stopping you from making the change?

The main 1–3 areas from categories 2 and 3 which would make a big difference to my health are:

....

....

....

....

The things that stop me from making these changes are:

....

....

....

....

What might the negative consequences be if you don't make these modifications? If I don't make these changes the negative consequences might be:

....

....

....

....

Consider the benefits you will gain from making these changes. If I made these changes the benefits for me would be:

....

....

....

....

Step 6

This exercise will only take 5–7 minutes. Visualize yourself making one of the changes from the list above.

1   Sit comfortably, close your eyes and relax.
2   Visualize or get a sense of yourself in the future doing one of the things you wrote on the list above. Be slightly distanced so that you have a picture of yourself doing it rather than feeling as if you are actually doing it now. (When you have a picture of yourself it is more likely to happen in the future.)
3   Make the image of yourself bright and colorful.
4   Bring in any other images which enable you to know that you are enjoying what you are doing, e.g. you may be with friends, you may look happy or you may be talking about what a good time you're having.
5   Get a sense that what you see yourself doing in the future has become a normal part of your life.
6   After you have seen yourself doing one of the things on the list, you can take the time to see yourself doing another one.
7   When you are ready, open your eyes and come back into the room.

You can do this exercise every day. It will reinforce the lifestyle areas you wish to adopt and make them more compelling. If you do this exercise every day for two weeks you will find you naturally start to make positive changes in your lifestyle. You can continue to do it until you have fulfilled all of your lifestyle aims.

Write the changes you have visualized on a sheet of paper and keep it next to your first list.

Step 7

Keep a third list next to this one. Write on the third list any areas you have not yet changed but would like to change in the future.

When you have changed the first one or two items on the lists, check back and see if some others have changed naturally. If you haven't changed them yet then go back and visualize yourself doing some of those things in the future.

Before finishing this final chapter I would like to wish you success with any changes you decide to make towards a healthier lifestyle. I'd like to remind you of two final points:

Firstly, the process of change takes time. Some changes take only a short time to carry out, but it may take years to truly integrate others into our lives. If we are patient with ourselves we may be surprised to find that we are making alterations quite effortlessly and find that we are naturally living a healthy lifestyle.

The second reminder is that we can't expect to be perfect – life is a process of growth and development and we can use our 'failures' as feedback for the future. Through trial and error we'll find out the best ways to live our lives to a healthy old age.

Good luck and good health!

Lifestyle Questionnaire

This questionnaire will give both specific and general advice on lifestyle.

Part 1

These are general areas which are basic to a healthy lifestyle. Place a cross against each one of these you do on a regular basis.

1 I eat meals, including breakfast, at regular times. For clarification read Chapter 2, page 43.
2 I generally eat correct proportions of food. For clarification read Chapter 2, page 18.
3 I tend to balance work and rest. For clarification read Chapters 4 and 6, pages 80 and 136.
4 I sleep for at least eight hours and go to bed at a regular time. For clarification read Chapter 4, page 102.
5 I exercise regularly and in a balanced way. For clarification read Chapter 4, page 87.
6 I tend to remain stable and not go through huge emotional ups and downs. For clarification read Chapter 3, page 52.
7 I'm careful to protect myself from the weather. For clarification read Chapter 5, page 111.

Part 2

This part of the questionnaire will enable us to gain more specific knowledge about our lifestyle:

Please note: This is only a guideline and is not meant to replace a professional diagnosis by a doctor or practitioner of Chinese medicine.

Am I Susceptible to Cold?

1   Do you dislike being out in cold weather?
2   Do you tend to huddle up to heaters and radiators?
3   Do you want to turn on the electric blanket or have a hot water bottle as soon as the temperature drops even slightly?
4   If you are out in the cold do you pass water more?
5   Do you crave holidays in sunny climates?

If the answer to at least three of these questions is Yes, you are more Cold than Hot.

Suggestions

Wrap up well against cold weather, bearing in mind the suggestions in Chapter 5 on protection against the cold. Avoid all Cold foods such as raw foods, ice cream and iced drinks and never eat food straight from the fridge. Allow food from the fridge to warm to room temperature. Avoid eating too much food from the 'Cold' or 'Cool' categories of the list on page 35 and take more Neutral and slightly Warming foods.

Am I Susceptible to Heat?

1   Do you get uncomfortably hot in warm weather?
2   Do you ever wake at night wanting to remove some of the bedcovers?
3   Do you tend to get restless when the room is too hot?
4   Do you find you need to wear fewer clothes than many of your friends?

If the answer to two or more of these questions is Yes then you are probably more Hot than Cold.

Suggestions

Be especially careful of the sun or if you are in very hot environments – bear in mind any suggestions from Chapter 5 about protecting yourself from the sun and heat. Avoid foods which are more heating in their nature such as curries, lamb, beef, coffee or alcohol – see page 35 for the rest of the list.

Temper heating foods with ones that have a cooling nature. Beware of any desire to drink iced drinks and other extremely cold foods. Allow Cold foods to warm to room temperature even if you are more Hot than Cold – we still need heat to digest our food.

Am I Prone to Retaining Dampness?

1 Do you feel worse in damp weather?
2 Do you easily bloat up in your abdomen or stomach?
3 Do you sometimes feel heavy in your limbs or head?
4 Do you often want to lie down?
5 Do you feel muzzy headed or lack concentration sometimes?

If the answer to three or more of these questions is Yes then you may be prone to retaining Dampness in your system.

Suggestions

Protect yourself from the Damp by following the suggestions in Chapter 5. Avoid dairy produce and other 'Damp' forming foods in your diet – see page 22. Try not to eat too many rich foods.

Am I too Dry?

1 Do you get thirsty easily?
2 Do you have a tendency to get dry skin?

3   Do you quite enjoy damp weather but hate dryness?
4   Do you easily get a dry cough?

If the answer to at least two of these questions is Yes then you may have a tendency towards Dryness.

Suggestions

Moisten a dry atmosphere with a humidifier. See advice on protecting yourself from Dryness in Chapter 5. Add moist foods to your diet such as porridge, soups and sauces. Dryness can also result from 'Blood Deficiency' (*see pages 25 and 229*).

Am I Affected by Wind?

1   Are you easily affected by changes in temperature, windy weather or drafts?
2   Do you ever have pains which move position or come and go?
3   Do you ever have itchy skin, painful ears, eyes, nose, sneezing or shivering when exposed to draughts or changes in temperature?
4   Do you ever have itching or prickling sensations in the skin?

If the answer to at least two of these questions is Yes you may easily be affected by Wind.

Suggestions

Cover your neck in windy weather. Wrap up warmly against changes in temperature. Notice if you are also Blood Deficient or Hot and follow instructions. Read about protecting yourself from Wind in Chapter 5.

Am I Blood Deficient?

1   Do your nails break easily?
2   Do you frequently get cramps or pins and needles in your limbs?
3   Do you easily get anxious, startle easily or have a poor memory?

4   Do you often find it hard to get off to sleep or do you sleep lightly?
5   Do you feel slightly light-headed when moving from sitting to standing?

If the answer to three or more of these questions is Yes then you are probably slightly Blood Deficient.

Suggestions

If you are vegetarian, consider including meat, fish or poultry in your diet. Also add more leafy green vegetables, beans and apricots, dates and figs. If you are over-anxious or emotionally sensitive, look at Chapter 3 on emotions. For women, if you are bleeding heavily during your period, you may need to get the help of Chinese medicine.

Have I a Tendency Towards Stomach and Spleen Qi Deficiency?

1   Do you often feel tired or tire towards the end of the day even without overdoing it?
2   Do you often crave sweet foods or fast foods rather than a nourishing diet?
3   If you're feeling tired do you find it hard to digest your food or easily get loose bowels?
4   Do you sometimes feel weak in your legs and prefer to sit down?

If the answer to at least two of these questions is Yes then you may have a tendency towards Qi Deficiency.

Suggestions

Eat appropriate amounts of high quality fresh food. Balance the proportions of the food you eat, bringing in more grains and vegetables to balance strong tasting foods. See Chapter 2, page 17. Do some exercise, but gentle exercise only.

Is my Life too Yang and Overactive?

1 Do you often work through your lunch-break without stopping?
2 Do you over-ride feelings of tiredness and carry on working?
3 Do you often feel obliged to work late?
4 If you are ill do you go back to work before you have fully convalesced?
5 Do you find you are continually juggling so many things that you never stop?

If you answered Yes to three or more of these questions then stop … you are probably in the habit of overworking. It may be difficult for you to stop and take notice.

Suggestions

Book in some time to look at your daily routine. Check that you're getting enough rest, breaks at work and time to nourish yourself. Book at least a small amount of rest time into your day. Read Chapter 4 for suggestions.

Is my Life too Yin and Static?

1 Do you spend a large proportion of the day sitting?
2 Do you feel tired even though you've been inactive?
3 Do you drive to work when it would be easy to cycle or walk?
4 Do you exercise less than once a week?
5 Do you feel sluggish and depressed much of the time?

If you answered Yes to three or more of these questions then assess ways of bringing exercise and activity into your day.

Suggestions

If you can't find a way to get exercise while you are working then put time aside out of working hours. Read Chapter 4 for suggestions.

Please note: If you have had a virus from which you have never recovered or if your Energy is extremely depleted then the above advice does not apply. You may have a post-viral condition. In this case visit a practitioner of Chinese medicine for specific advice.

Are my Emotions Affecting my Health?

1 Have you been under any prolonged or intense strain in your life which you still haven't recovered from?
2 Do you find it difficult to express your negative emotions?
3 Do you have a tendency to strong emotional feelings which you can't easily shrug off?
4 Is your current lifestyle causing you to feel stressed?

If the answer to at least two of these questions is Yes then your emotions may be affecting your health.

Suggestions

Re-read Part 2 of Chapter 4 on ways of dealing with emotions. Look for a suggestion which suits you and try it for a month. Notice whether you feel healthier or less strained as a result. If your life is stressed read Chapter 4 on work, rest and exercise and Chapter 6 on constitution.

How Strong is my Constitution?

1 Do you regularly feel totally depleted in energy?
2 Do you have signs of premature aging such as: graying hair, baldness, drying skin or wrinkles?
3 Have you had difficulty conceiving, continuous backaches, an early menopause if you are a woman or impotence or a low sperm count if you are a man?
4 Are you constantly getting infections and do you invariably catch other people's colds and flu?
5 Have you got small ears and short earlobes, or a weak jaw line?

If the answer is Yes to three or more of these questions then you may have slightly weakened Jing.

Suggestions

Follow the guidelines in this book about work, rest and exercise in Chapter 4 and constitution in Chapter 6. Eat a healthy diet. Practise Qigong exercises.

Some Basic Recipes

When measuring out grains or beans, you can use a standard teacup or mug, as long as you use the same size throughout the recipe.

Cooking Grains

Rice

Serves 3–4

1 cup of rice
2 cups of water
Sea salt to taste

1   Rinse rice thoroughly and place in a heavy pan with the water. Cover and boil.
2   Simmer for about 30 minutes or until all the water is absorbed.
3   Do not stir the rice.

Rice is tasty with soya sauce or tahini, which is made from sesame seeds, or with beans or lentils.

Barley
Serves 3–4

> *1 cup of barley*
> *3 cups of water*
> *1 tbsp of oil*
> *sea salt to taste*

1   Soak barley for about 15 minutes. Pour off the water and rinse thoroughly.
2   Place barley, water, oil and salt in a pan. Cover and boil.
3   Simmer for $1\frac{1}{4}$–$1\frac{1}{2}$ hours.
4   Stir occasionally while cooking.

Barley can be used in soups, stews or as a breakfast cereal.

Millet
Serves 2–3

> *1 cup of millet*
> *3 cups of water*
> *sea salt to taste*

1   Rinse millet thoroughly.
2   Roast millet in a pan until it is slightly brown and has a nutty taste.
3   Place in a heavy pan with the water and salt. Cover and boil.
4   Simmer for about 20 minutes.

Millet can be mixed with rice or vegetables or taken in soups and stews.

Couscous (cracked wheat)
Serves 3–4

> *1 cup of couscous*
> *approximately $2\frac{1}{2}$ cups of water*
> *sea salt to taste*

1 Put couscous in a bowl and cover with boiling water.
2 Cover the bowl and leave for 10-15 minutes until water is absorbed.
3 'Fluff up' with a fork and serve.

This can be served hot or cold. Used in soups or stews or can be used in a dessert.

Cooking Beans

All beans, except lentils and split peas, need to be soaked overnight. This cuts the cooking time and is said to remove any gas from them. Do not add salt until they have finished cooking as salt prevents them from becoming tender. Beans can be eaten by themselves or mixed in a dish with rice or other grains. These recipes serve 3-4 people.

Adzuki beans
Cover with water and soak overnight. Wash thoroughly and add 1 cup of adzuki beans to 3 cups of water. Simmer for $1\frac{1}{2}$-2 hours until soft.

Black-eyed beans
Cover with water and soak overnight. Wash thoroughly and add 1 cup of black-eyed beans to 3 cups of water. Simmer for $1\frac{1}{2}$-2 hours until soft.

Chickpeas (garbanzos)
Cover with water and soak overnight. Wash thoroughly and add 1 cup of chickpeas (garbanzos) to 3 cups of water. Simmer for 1-2 hours until soft.

Soya beans
Cover with water and soak overnight. Wash thoroughly and add 1 cup of soya beans to 3 cups of water. Simmer for at least 3 hours until soft.

Haricot beans
Cover with water and soak overnight. Wash thoroughly and add 1 cup of haricot beans to 3 cups of water. Simmer for 1-2 hours until soft.

Kidney beans
Cover with water and soak overnight. Wash thoroughly and add 1 cup of kidney beans to 3 cups of water. Simmer for 1½–2 hours until soft.

Split peas
No need to soak. Boil 1 cup of split peas to 2 cups of water for about 30–45 minutes.

Lentils
No need to soak. Boil 1 cup of lentils to 2 cups of water for about 30–40 minutes.

Sprouting Beans
Many beans, grains and seeds can be sprouted including wheat, rice, mung beans, alfalfa seeds, chickpeas (garbanzos), whole lentils and sunflower seeds. They are easy to sprout and nourishing to eat.
To sprout:

1 Take 2 tablespoons of beans, seeds or grains and place in a jar.
2 Cover with water and place in a warm dark place overnight or until they begin to sprout.
3 Drain and rinse thoroughly 3–4 times every day until they are sprouted to about 1–2 inches (3–5 cm) long.

These can be used in sandwiches or mixed with grains or other vegetables.

Cooking Seaweed

Seaweed is traditionally used in the Orient and is most commonly used by the Japanese. It is especially useful for vegetarians to enrich their diet as it is rich in minerals. Here are basic recipes for wakame, hiziki, nori, kombu and arame, some common types of seaweed. These seaweeds are usually available from health food shops.

Wakame

Wash thoroughly. Use a piece 1 inch square per person. Add to cold water and soak for 5 minutes. Chop to the required size. Add to soups and stews. As well as adding this to soups and stews it can be eaten alone or with vegetable dishes.

Hiziki

This is a tasty black stringy seaweed. Wash thoroughly then soak for 1 hour. Squeeze out the water and save it. Fry in a little oil for a few minutes. Add the soaking water that you have saved and simmer until tender. This can be eaten alone or sautéed with vegetables like carrots or onions.

Kombu

Wash thoroughly. Take a piece one inch square per person. Soak for 15 minutes. Can use this with beans to tenderize them and prevent gas.

Nori (also known in the West as laver)

This comes in thin sheets and is dried. It can be toasted over a flame and then sprinkled on food or can be dipped into cold water and wrapped around rice to make rice balls.

Arame

Wash thoroughly. Use a handful the size of a ping pong ball for two people. Fry with onions or soak for a few minutes then add to casseroles or stews.

Tabbouleh

Serves 4–6

175g (6oz/1 cup) bulgar wheat or couscous
100g (4oz/1 cup) onion, finely chopped
75g (3oz/1½–2 cups) fresh parsley, finely chopped
25g (1oz/½ cup) fresh mint, finely chopped
2 tomatoes, finely chopped
½ cucumber, finely chopped

½ tsp ground black pepper

4 tbsp lemon juice

1　Soak the bulgar or couscous in cold water for 2–2½ hours. Drain in a sieve lined with a clean cloth. Twist the cloth around the bulgar and squeeze to remove all the moisture.

2　Turn into a large bowl and knead in the onion by hand for a couple of minutes.

3　Mix the remaining ingredients into the bulgar mixture before serving.

Warm puy lentil and smoked salmon salad

Serves 3–4

250g (8oz/1½ cups) puy lentils

1 onion, roughly chopped

1 carrot, cut into short sticks

1 lime, juice

1 tbsp sesame oil

1 tbsp walnut oil

2 garlic cloves, finely chopped

salt

pepper

100g (3½oz/½ cup) smoked salmon, chopped

1　Put the lentils into a large saucepan and cover with cold water (up to the lentils and then as much again), bring to the boil. Simmer for 20 minutes.

2　Add the onion and carrot. Simmer for a further 20 minutes until the lentils have absorbed all the water (add a few drops of water if necessary).

3　In a separate serving dish, mix the lime juice, oils, garlic and seasoning. Add the hot lentil mixture and stir.

4　Allow to cool slightly before adding the smoked salmon just before serving.

Chickpea (garbanzo) and ginger spheres

Serves 2–4

180g (12oz/2 cups) chickpeas (garbanzos)

2 tbsp fresh rosemary

sea salt to taste

2 egg whites

1 tbsp ginger, freshly grated

ground black pepper

1 medium onion, chopped

160ml (6fl oz/½ cup) olive oil

455g (1lb/2 cups) tomatoes, chopped

1 Soak the chickpeas (garbanzos) overnight, then discard the water.
2 Place in a saucepan, cover with fresh water and bring to the boil (remove any froth which is produced).
3 Add the rosemary and half a teaspoon of sea salt.
4 Cook until tender (approximately 60 minutes).
5 Remove from heat and drain.
6 Place in a food processor and turn into pulp while still warm.
7 When cool, add the slightly beaten egg whites, ginger and ground pepper.
8 Meanwhile place the onion, oil and tomatoes into a saucepan with seasoning and 280ml (10fl oz/1½ cups) water and cook for 10 minutes, stirring frequently.
9 Now take a small amount of chickpea (garbanzo) mixture, shape into balls and place into the simmering tomato/onion sauce.
10 If the spheres are not completely covered, add a little boiling water to thin the sauce.
11 Bring to the boil and cook for 10–15 minutes or until the water has evaporated.

Pea and lentil loaf

Serves 4

100g (3½oz/½ cup) split peas

100g (3½oz/½ cup) brown lentils

1 tbsp chopped parsley

½ tsp dried mixed herbs

500ml (18fl oz/2⅓ cups) stock or vegetable water

2 tbsp olive oil

1 medium onion, chopped

2 tbsp green (bell) peppers, chopped

2 medium carrots, diced

2 sticks celery, chopped

1 garlic clove, crushed

1 egg, beaten

4 tbsp bran flakes

60g (2oz/⅓ cup) ham, chopped

1 Preheat the oven to 190°C (375°F/Gas Mark 5).
2 Cook the lentils and peas in the stock, with the herbs, until the liquid has been absorbed and the pulses are soft.
3 Heat the oil in a large pan, add the remaining vegetables and garlic, cover and cook on a low heat for 20–25 minutes, stirring occasionally.
4 Stir in the lentil mixture, add the egg, bran flakes, chopped ham and season.
5 Grease a 450g (1lb) loaf tin, add the mixture, cover with foil and bake for 40–45 minutes.

Chicken casserole

Serves 4

300g (10½oz/1½ cups) brown rice

300g (10½oz/1⅓ cups) chicken, cut into strips

2 medium onions

340g (12oz/2½ cups) mixed vegetables

1 tsp curry powder

1 tbsp soy sauce

salt and pepper to taste

1 tbsp boiling chicken stock

2 tbsp chopped parsley

1 Preheat the oven to 180°C (350°F/Gas Mark 4).
2 In a casserole dish, mix the rice, meat and vegetables together.
3 Mix the curry powder, soy sauce and seasoning with the stock and add to the casserole dish.
4 Cover and cook for 1¼–1½ hours, until the liquid has been absorbed.
5 Stir in the parsley, leaving a little to garnish before serving.

Lamb and bean stew

Serves 4

225g (8oz/1 cup) stewing lamb

2 tsp olive oil

2 onions

200g (7oz/1 cup) haricot beans, soaked (see page 222)

375ml (13fl oz/1⅔ cups) water

salt and pepper

2 carrots

200g (7oz/1½ cups) swede or turnip, chopped

3 tsp wholemeal flour

1 Remove any excess fat from the lamb. Cut the lamb into small cubes.
2 Heat the oil in a pan and fry the onion until golden. Move the onions to one side of the pan before adding the lamb. Fry until lightly browned.
3 Add the beans, water, seasoning and boil for 10 minutes. Reduce heat and simmer for 1–1¼ hours.
4 Add the carrots and swede (or turnips) and cook for a further ½–¾ hour, until tender.
5 Blend the flour with 2 teaspoons of water, add a little gravy from the lamb and stir into the stew.
6 Cook for a further 5 minutes before serving.

Glossary

Blood
Blood nourishes and moistens the body and allows the Spirit to be settled and calm.

Blood Deficiency
This is a general term used when the Blood is no longer able to carry out the functions listed above. Blood Deficiency leads to symptoms such as dry skin, insomnia, dizziness, tinnitus, numbness, scanty periods, poor memory, a tendency to startle easily and anxiety. Symptoms specific to the organ which has become Blood Deficient will also manifest.

Blood Stagnation
This is a term used when the Blood is 'stuck' and unable to move properly. It can cause symptoms such as blood clots, purple veins and/or severe, fixed, stabbing pain.

Cold
A climatic cause of disease which can manifest with symptoms such as aversion to cold, cold limbs, contraction of the tendons, thin, watery, clear discharges and severe pain relieved by warmth and aggravated by cold.

Damp
A climatic cause of disease which can manifest with symptoms such as aversion to damp or humidity, heavy limbs, heavy head, no appetite, a stuffy

feeling in the chest or stomach area, recurrent dirty discharges or secretions and/or depressions.

Dryness
A climatic cause of disease which can manifest with symptoms such as a dry throat, dry mouth, dry nose, dry lips, dry skin, dry stools and/or scanty urination.

Heart Functions
Some important functions of the Heart are 1) to 'house' the Spirit and 2) to circulate the Blood.

Heat
A climatic cause of disease which can manifest with symptoms such as an aversion to heat, sweating, dark-scanty urine, headache, dry lips and thirst.

Kidney Functions
Some important functions of the Kidneys are to 1) store 'Jing' or constitutional Qi and 2) to control the water functions in the body.

Liver Functions
Some important functions of the Liver are to 1) allow the Qi to flow smoothly throughout the body and 2) to 'store' the Blood.

Lung Functions
Some important functions of the Lungs are to 1) control our ability to breath and take in Qi via the Lungs and 2) to disperse defensive or 'Wei' Qi to the skin, thus protecting us from the effects of the climate.

Phlegm
Phlegm arises from stagnation of the body fluids. It can cause symptoms such as mucus in the Lungs, nodules on joints, kidney or gall stones and/or lumps under the skin. If it blocks the Heart orifices it can cause some forms of mental illness.

Qi
(Pronounced 'chi'). Usually translated as 'energy'. Qi moves, transforms, protects, holds and warms everything in our body.

Qi Deficiency

This is a general term used when the Qi has become weak. When the Qi is deficient it can no longer perform the functions listed above and symptoms of general weakness and tiredness will arise. Symptoms specific to the organ which has become deficient will also manifest.

Qi Stagnation

This is a general term used when the Qi is not moving properly. Because Qi is very refined and light, Qi stagnation will often come and go according to our moods or with movement. It will cause many symptoms including ones which appear and disappear, distending pain which moves around, symptoms which are better with massage, mood swings and/or depression.

Spirit

The Chinese describe the Spirit as the part of us which is responsible for our overall sense of purpose and identity. A 'settled' spirit also allows us to think clearly and have good concentration, memory and sleep.

Spleen Functions

Some important functions of the Spleen are to 1) transform and move food, drink and our thoughts; 2) to rule over all digestive functions and 3) to keep the Blood in the blood vessels.

Stomach Function

One important function of the Stomach is to digest or 'rot and ripen' food and drink.

Wind

A climatic cause of disease which can manifest as rapidly changing symptoms, symptoms which move around, symptoms which affect the top part of the body and ones which affect the Lung first. Other manifestations can be itching, tremors, convulsions and/or numbness.

Yang

More active energy. Some Yang qualities are heat, dryness, movement, and an upward direction.

Yin

More passive energy. Some Yin qualities are coldness, wetness, stillness and sinking down.

Yin/Yang Balance

Yin and Yang are opposites as well as constantly interacting. These two qualities balance each other. When out of balance they cause disharmony in the body, mind and spirit, leading to illness.

Notes

Introduction

1 Table 3, *The 1991 Census Limiting Long-term Illness for Great Britain*, HMSO, 1993.

Chapter 1 Why a Healthy Lifestyle?

1 Inglis, Brian. *The Diseases of Civilisation*, Granada, 1981.

Chapter 2 The Secret of Healthy Eating

1 Bruce, Ake. 'Nutrition and Human Health', *Environment Lifestyle and Health*. A report from the European Workshop on the Environment Lifestyle and Health, Stromsted. Swedish Council for Planning and Co-ordinating Research, September 1991.

2 Steen, Bertil. 'Social Environment and Health in the Elderly', *Environment Lifestyle and Health*. A report from the European Workshop on the Environment Lifestyle and Health, Stromsted. Swedish Council for Planning and Co-ordinating Research, 1991.

3 Buss, D. H. 'How Healthy is the British Diet?', *Journal of the Institute of Health Education*, Volume 33, No. 1, 1995.

4 The Mediterranean diet was typical of that eaten in Crete and much of the rest of Greece and Southern Italy in the early 1960s. It contained an abundance of fruit, vegetables, breads and other cereals, potatoes, beans, nuts and seeds.

Olive oil was the principle source of fat. Dairy products were kept low. Fish and poultry was taken in low to moderate amounts and red meat in low quantities too. Zero to four eggs were taken per week. Wine was also consumed in low to moderate amounts.

5 The Japanese diet contains large amounts of rice, soya products, vegetables and fruit as well as some seaweed. A limited amount of red meat is eaten. Instead of red meat more fish, poultry and seafood are taken. The diet also contains few dairy foods, eggs and sugar.

6 This is not necessarily the case now since proportions in the diet have changed.

7 Willet, W.C.; Sacks, F.; Trichopoulou, A.; and Drescher, G. 'The Mediterranean Diet Pyramid. A Cultural Model for Healthy Eating', *American Journal of Clinical Nutrition*, Volume 61, 1995.

8 Ibid.

9 *The Balance of Good Health*, the Department of Health and the Ministry of Agriculture Fisheries and Food, 1994. They now suggest a diet using these quantities of foods.

10 Schmidt, T.F.H. and Noack, R.H. 'Homeostasis', *Lifestyle Changes – A Public Health Perspective*, November 1994.

11 Flaws, Bob. *Arisal of the Clear*, Blue Poppy Press, 1993. Page 12.

12 Ibid. Page 10.

13 Quote from *Clin Ortho Related Res*, 1980; 152: 35 from Kitty Champion, 'Dial M for Milk', *What Doctors Don't Tell You*, Volume 5, No. 1.

14 Taggart, Helen M. and Connor, Sara E. 'The Relation of Exercise Habits to Health Beliefs and Knowledge about Osteoporosis', *The Journal of American College Health*, Volume 44, 1995, pages 127–30.

15 Kushi, Lenart and Willet. 'Health Implications of a Mediterranean Diet in the Light of Contemporary Knowledge of Meat, Wine Fats and Oil', *American Journal of Clinical Nutrition*, Volume 61, 1995, pages 1416S–27S.

16 Godfrey, K.; Robinson, S.; Barker, D.J.P.; Osmond, C. and Cox, V. 'Maternal Nutrition in Early and Late Pregnancy in Relation to Placental and Fetal Growth', *British Medical Journal*, 17 February 1996.

17 The Chinese say that a very pale tongue is also a sign of Blood Deficiency.

18 For more information on food combinations read Lappe, *Diet for a Small Planet*, published by Ballantyne, 1978.

19 *Living Earth*, No 188, October 1995. For more information contact The Soil Association, 86 Colston Street, Bristol BS1 5BB.

20 *Verbal Communication*, June 1997.

21 Hicks, Angela. *Principles of Chinese Medicine*, London, Thorsons, 1996

22 Ibid.

23 My thanks to Gordon Peck for most of these suggestions which were given at a talk he gave on Dietary Therapy. He is also the editor of the book *Chinese Dietary Therapy* published by Churchill Livingstone, 1995.

Chapter 3 The Secret of Balancing Our Emotions

1 Stone, A.; Cox, D.; Valdimarsdottir, H.; Jandorf, L. and Neale, J. 'Secretory IgA Antibody is Associated with Daily Mood', *Journal of Personality and Social Psychology*, Volume 52, May 1987, pages 988–93.

2 Peterson, Christopher; Seligmam, Martin; and Vaillant, George. 'Pessimistic Explanatory Style is a Risk Factor for Physical Illness: A 35-year Longitudinal Study', *Journal of Personality and Social Psychology*, Volume 55. No 1, 1988, pages 23–7.

3 Gail Ironson, *et al.* 'The Effects of Anger on Left Ventricular Fraction in Coronary Artery Disease', *American Journal of Cardiology*, 1992, pages 281–5.

4 Research carried out by National Opinion Poll for *Bella Magazine*, November 1996.

5 McEwen, Bruce and Stellar, Elliot. 'Stress and Metastasis', *Archives of Internal Medicine*, September 27th 1993, pages 2093–2101.

6 Rabin, B.; Cohen, S.; Ganguli, R.; Lysle, D.; and Cunnick, J. 'Bidirectional Interaction between the Central Nervous System and the Immune System', *Critical Reviews and Immunology*, Volume 9, Issue 4, 1989, page 298.

7 Bartrop, R.W.; Lazarus, L.; Luckhurst, E.; Kiloh, C.G. and Penny, R. 'Depressed Lymphocyte Function after Bereavement', *Lancet*, 16 April 1977, pages 834–7.

8 McEwen, Bruce and Stellar, Elliot. 'Stress and Metastasis', *Archives of Internal Medicine*, 27 September 1993, page 2097.

9 *Huang Qi Nei Jing (Yellow Emperor's Classic of Internal Medicine)*. There are two parts to this book. This is in the part called the Su Wen or Simple questions, Chapter 39. There are many translations.

10 Zhengcai, Liu. *The Mystery of Longevity*, Beijing, Foreign Languages Press, 1990, page 34.

11 Cousins, Norman. *Anatomy of an Illness*, W.W. Norton, 1996.

12 Zhengcai, Liu. *The Mystery of Longevity*, Beijing, Foreign Languages Press, 1990, page 32.

13 For more ways of reframing see *Reframing* by Richard Bandler and John Grinder. Published by Real People Press, 1983.

14 Taylor, S.E. and Brown, J.D. 'Illusion and Wellbeing. A Social Perspective on Dental Health', *The Psychological Bulletin*, Volume 2, 1988, pages 193–210.

15 Wilhelm, Richard translation. Hexagon 'Obstruction', *I Ching (Book of Changes)*, Routledge and Kegan Paul, 1983, page 152.

16 These perceptual positions were developed by Robert Dilts and are used in Neuro Linguistic Programming (NLP). For more on NLP read *The Principles of NLP* by Joseph O'Connor and Ian McDermott, published by Thorsons, 1996. Perceptual positions are written about on page 26.

17 Linda Chih-Ling Koo. *Nourishment of Life*, Commercial Press Ltd, 1987, page 111.

18 Tien Tai Monks. Verbal Communication from Dr Shen Hongxun in 1995. Dr Shen teaches Qigong exercises Tai Chi Chuan and meditation.

19 Linda Chih-Ling Koo. *Nourishment of Life*, Commercial Press Ltd, 1987, page 119.

20 For more about this see Angela and John Hicks, *Healing Your Emotions*, Thorsons, 1999.

Chapter 4 The Secret of How to Work, Rest and Exercise

1 Armstrong, Neil and McManus, Alison. 'Children's Fitness and Physical Activity', *The British Journal of Physical Education*, Spring 1994.

2 Chollar, Susan. 'Psychological Benefits of Exercise', American Health, June 1995.

3 Taggart, H.M. and Connor, S.E. 'The Relation of Exercise Habits to Health Beliefs and Knowledge about Osteoporosis', *The Journal of American College Health*, Volume 44, November 1995.

4 Rowland, Thomas W. *Exercise and Children's Health Human Kinetics Books*, 1989, Chapter 6, page 106.

5 Herbert, William G. and Ribisl, Paul M. *Exercise Lite Meaning and Implication*, Parks and Recreation, 1995.

6 Frantzis, Bruce K, *Opening the Energy Gates of Your Body*, North Atlantic Books, Berkeley California, 1993

7 Ibid. Chapter 3, pages 45–60.

8 My thanks to Qigong master Zhi Xing Wang for teaching me the exercise on which this is based.

9 Ornstein, Robert and Sobel, David. *Healthy Pleasures*, Addison Wesley, 1989, page 120.

10 Ibid. Page 119.

11 Adapted from an exercise in *300 Questions on Qigong Exercises*, compiled by Lin Housheng and Luo Peiyu. Guangdong Science and Technology Press, 1994, page 67.

12 Pillsbury, Barbara L. K. 'Doing the Month', *Health and Disease*, Open University Press, 1980, pages 19–24.

Chapter 5 The Secret of Protecting Ourselves from the Environment

1 Gauquelin, Michael. *How Atmospheric Conditions Affect Your Health*, ASI publishers Inc., 1989, page 62.

2 Ibid. Page 39.

3 Ibid. Page 99.

Chapter 6 The Secret of Respecting Our Constitution

1 Maciocia, Giovanni. 'The Foundations of Chinese Medicine', Churchill Livingstone, taken from the *Classic of the Simple Girl*, 1989, page 136.

2 For more on breathing see *Relaxing into your Being* by Bruce K Frantzis.

3 For more on posture and standing meditation see, Frantzis, Bruce K, *Opening the Energy Gates of Your Body*, North Atlantic Books, Berkeley California, 1993

4 For more on Qigong read *The Principles of Chinese Medicine* by Angela Hicks. Published by Thorsons, 1996, chapter 6.

5 Zhengcai, Liu. *The Mystery of Longevity*, Beijing, Foreign Languages Press, 1990, page 77.

6 Ibid. Page 55.

Chapter 8 Where do I Start?

1 Chollar, Susan. 'The Psychological Benefits of Exercise', *American Health*, June 1995, pages 73–5.

2 Breslow, L. and Breslow N. 'Health Practises and Disability: Some Evidence from Alameda County', *Preventative Medicine*, 1993, pages 86–95.

Reading List

Chih-Ling Koo, Linda. *Nourishment of Life – Health in Chinese Society*, Hong Kong, The Commercial Press Ltd.

Flaws, Bob. *Arisal of the Clear – A Simple Guide to Healthy Eating According to Traditional Chinese Medicine*, Blue Poppy Press.

Flaws, Bob. *Imperial Secrets of Health and Longevity*, Blue Poppy Press.

Frantzis Bruce Kumar – *Opening the Energy Gates of Your Body*, North Atlantic Books, Berkeley California.

Frantzis Bruce Kumar - Relaxing into your Being, (available from brucefrantzis@energyarts.com)

Housheng, Lin and Peiyu, Luo. *Three Hundred Questions on Qigong Exercises*, Guangdong Science and Technology Press.

MacRitchie, James. *Chi Kung*, Element.

Dr Mann and the Oxford Dietetic Group. *The Diabetics' Diet Book*, Martin Dunitz.

McDermott, Ian and Joseph O'Connor, Joseph. *NLP and Health*, London, Thorsons.

Leggett, Daverick. *Helping Ourselves*, Meridian Press.

Leggett Daverick, *Recipes for Self Healing*, Meridian Press.

Ornstein, Robert and Sobel, David. *Healthy Pleasures*, Addison Wesley Publishing Company, Inc.

Qingnan, Zeng. *Methods of Traditional Chinese Health Care*, Beijing, Foreign Languages Health.

Weiser Cornell, Ann. *The Power of Focusing – A Practical Guide to Emotional Self-healing*, New Harbinger Publications.

Various Chinese authors. *Practical Ways to Good Health through Traditional Chinese Medicine*, China Reconstructs Press.

Zhengcai, Lui. *The Mystery of Longevity*, Beijing, Foreign Languages Press.

Useful Addresses

If you wish to find out more about any Chinese medicine treatments or to buy specialist Chinese medicine books you can phone, write or e-mail the contacts listed below.

UK

Acupuncture

• **British Acupuncture Council**
Park House
63 Jeddo Road
London
W12 9HQ
Tel: 020 8735 0400
E-mail: info@acupuncture.org.uk
Website: www.acupuncture.org.uk

Herbs

• **Register of Chinese Herbal Medicine**
Garden Studios
11-15 Betterton Street
Covent Garden
London
WC2H 9BP
Tel: 07000 790332
E-mail: info@rchm.co.uk
Website: www.rchm.co.uk

Tui na massage

Sarah Pritchard
48 Lockhurst Street
London
E5 0AP
Tel: 020 8986 3200

Rosie Grandige
Westminster University Chinese
   Medicine Department
115 New Cavendish Road
London
WC1 8JD
Tel: 020 7911 5000 Ext 3724
Website: www.westminster.ac.uk.

Qigong

Chris Chappell
Skychord Foundation
Unit 9
170 Brick Lane
London
E1 6RU
Tel: 020 7247 1399
E-mail Chris@skychord.co.uk
Website: www.skychord.co.uk

Graham Kennedy
c/o The College of Integrated Chinese
   Medicine
19 Castle Street
Reading
Berkshire RG1 7SB
Tel: 0118 950 8880

Gio Maschio
63 Richmond Avenue
London
N1 0LX
Tel: 020 7700 5819
E-mail: gio@hotmail.com

Robert McAlpine
50 Windsor Terrace
South Gosforth
Newcastle-upon-Tyne
NE3 1YL
Tel: 0191 285 1941

Nguyen Tinh Thong
1 Marlborough Studio
12 Finchley Road
St John's Wood
London
NW8 6EB
Tel: 020 7586 6543

BuQi College UK
28 Withleigh Road
Knowle
Bristol
BS4 2LQ
Tel: 0117 907 3380

Zhi Xing Wang and Wu Zhendi
Chinese Heritage
Flat 3
15 Dawson Place,
London
W2
Tel: 0171 229 7187

Specialist books on Chinese Medicine

- **Acumedic**

101-105 Camden High Street

London

NW1 7JN

Tel: 020 7388 6704

E-mail: info@acumedic.com

Website: www.acumedic.com

- **East-West Herbs**

Langston Priory Mews

Kingham

Oxfordshire

OX7 6UP

Tel: 01608 658862

Fax: 01608 658816

E-mail: sales@healthpack.ssnet.co.uk

- **Harmony Medical Distribution**

629 High Road

Leytonstone

London

E11 4PA

Tel: 020 8518 7337

E-mail: harmony@tcm.org.uk

Website: www.tcm.org.uk

Herbal suppliers

- **East-West Herbs**

Langston Priory Mews

Kingham

Oxfordshire

OX7 6UP

Tel: 01608 658862

Fax: 01608 658816

E-mail: sales@healthpack.ssnet.co.uk

- **Mayway Herbal Emporium**

43 Waterside Trading Estate

Trumpers Way

Hanwell

London

W7 2QD

Tel: 020 8893 6873

Fax: 020 8893 6874

E-mail: admin@mayway.demon.co.uk

Website: www.mayway.demon.co.uk.

- **Oxford Medical Supplies Ltd**

Unit 11/12

Horcott Industrial Estate

Fairford

Gloucester

GL7 4BX

E-mail: ewan@oxfordms.co.uk

If you wish to find out more information from the author you can contact her at:
The College of Integrated Chinese
   Medicine
19 Castle Street
Reading
Berkshire
RG1 7SB
Tel: 0118 950 8880
E-mail: info@cicm.org.uk
Website: www.cicm.org.uk

AUSTRALIA
Acupuncture and herbs

• National Academic Standards
Committee for TCM
c/o Australian Acupuncture and
Chinese Medicine Association Ltd.
PO Box 5142
West End
Queensland 4104
Tel: 07 3846 5866

Qigong

• **Qigong Association of Australia**
458 White Horse Road
Surrey Hills
Victoria 3127
Tel: 03 836 6961

USA
Acupuncture and herbs

• **Council of Colleges of Acupuncture
and Oriental Medicine**
1010 Wayne Avenue
Suite 1270
Silver Spring
MD 20910
Tel: 301 608 9175
Website: www.ccaom.org

• **Acupuncture and Oriental Medicine
Alliance**
14637 Starr Road SE
Olalla
Washington 98359
Tel: 253 851 6896
Fax: 253 851 6883
Website: www.AcuAll.org

• **National Commission for Certified
Acupuncturists and Oriental Medicine
(NCCAOM)**
11 Canal Center Plaza Suite 3000
Alexandria
Virginia 22314
Tel: 703 548 9004
Website: www.nccaom.org

Qigong

Bruce Frantzis
Energy Arts
PO Box 99
Fairfax
CA 94978-0099
Tel: 415 454 5243
Website: www.energyarts.com

Bernie Langan
Taoist Internal Arts
Studio 813
San Pablo Avenue
Albany
CA 94706
Tel: 510 527 7760

Bill Ryan Brookline Tai Chi
1615 Beacon Street
Brookline
MA 02146 4602
Tel: 617 277 2972

Frank Allen
WuTang Physical Cultural Association
7 1/2 Second Avenue
3rd Floor
New York
NY 10003
Tel: 212 533 1751

Ed Ware
New York City
NY
Tel: 212 673 1361

Susan Kansky
Integrated Healing LLC
3370 N Hayden Road
Appt 123 PMB 524
Scotsdale
AZ 85251
Tel: 480 947 5161

Kurt Miyajima
Hawaii
USA
Tel: 808 573 8876

Specialist books on Chinese medicine

• **Redwing Reviews**
Redwing Book Company
44 Linden Street
Brookline
MA 02146
Tel: 617 738 4664
Orders: (USA) 800 873 3946
Fax: 617 738 4620

Herbal Suppliers

- **East-West Herbs USA**
6400 Hollis Street
Suite 14
Emeryville
CA 94608
Tel: 1800 575 8526
Fax: 510 652 2812

- **Crane Enterprises**
745 Falmouth Road
Mashpee
M 02649
Tel: 1800 227 4118
Fax: 508 539 2369

CANADA
Acupuncture

- **Toronto School of Traditional Chinese Medicine**
2010 Eglinton Avenue West
Suite 302
Toronto
ON
M6E 2KE
Tel: 416 782 9682
Email: info@tstcm.com
Website: www.tstcm.com

Qigong

Choco Chiswell
Appartment 106
527 Commodore Road
Vancouver
BC
V5Z 4G5
Tel: 604 872 3400
E-mail: ifschoco@hotmail.com

Herbal Suppliers

- **Energick Inc.**
1331 Boulevard Ste-foy
Longueuil
Quebec
J4K 1X8
Tel: 514 677 1640
Fax: 514 677 5841

- **Eastern Currents**
5621 Dunbar Street
Vancouver
BC
B6N 1W5
Tel: 604 263 5042
Fax: 604 261 8700

Index

Healing Your Emotions

Discover Your Element Type and Change Your Life

Angela Hicks and John Hicks

Chinese Traditional Medicine has long understood the connection between a positive outlook on life and our physical health. Our bodies manifest our emotions – frustration and anger can strain the heart, and worry can weaken the immune system.

Grounded in the Chinese Five Elements theory, *Healing Your Emotions* is packed with practical, powerful exercises to create balance, working with the Elements that rule crucial parts of our body, personality and emotions. Identify your Constitutional type and learn how to:

- enjoy better health now, and in the future
- identify and deal with the emotions which stop you being healthy
- discover your Constitutional type and create balance within
- enhance your self-awareness, develop stability and your inner sense of worth.

Let this book help you to transform anger, conquer fear, release sadness and break the worry habit – and restore health and well-being.

Angela and John Hicks are joint principals of The College of Integrated Chinese Medicine in Reading, England. They have practised and taught Chinese Medicine for over 20 years, and are both Master Practitioners of Neuro-Linguistic Programming.

ISBN: 0 7225 3728 X

Nine Ways to Body Wisdom

Blending Natural Therapies to Nourish Body, Emotions and Soul

Jennifer Harper

Nine Ways to Body Wisdom skilfully blends the best of traditional Eastern medicine and Western natural therapies to create a powerful new way of working with your body.

The Nine Ways of:
- nutrition
- herbs and spices
- exercise
- reflexology
- acupressure
- aromatherapy
- flower remedies
- affirmations, and
- meditations

combine to form the perfect self-treatment system.

Jennifer Harper N.D., Ph.D. is a qualified naturopathic doctor and herbalist and runs a successful clinical practice. She is also a popular broadcaster and media columnist.

Develop your own personal health plan you can follow throughout the year!

ISBN: 0 7225 3368 3

The Big Book of Ch'i

An Exploration of Energy, Form and Spirit

Paul Wildish

This beautifully illustrated book takes a fascinating look at the origins of 'ch'i' – our 'living essence' and the vital energy behind healing practices like reiki, chi kung, acupuncture and shiatsu. When this vital force is sluggish or becomes blocked, our health suffers; these ancient Eastern healing practices were developed to clear such energy blocks and to restore harmony within the body. Martial arts, like tai chi and aikido, use this same vital energy for self-protection and health promotion through exercise.

Paul Wildish, a martial arts expert and a senior instructor for the British Aikido Association, has studied aikido, shiatsu and reiki. In *The Big Book of Ch'i* he introduces these traditional ways to awaken this energy force and fulfil our true potential.

ISBN: 0 7225 3852 9 (HB)
      0 00 710013 2 (PB)